THE COLLEGE
COOKBOOK

THE COLLEGE COOKBOOK

REVISED EDITION

Geri Harrington

Charles Scribner's Sons / New York

ACKNOWLEDGMENTS

This book was really written by the college students who generously shared with me their problems, solutions, and experience in order to help other students in a similar situation. Without them, there wouldn't have been a college cookbook.

I would especially like to thank the following students whose recipes appear in this book: Gayle Adler, James Adler, Jeffrey Travis Atwood, Deborah Bachtel, Peggy Barlett, Jodi Bernstein, Bill Blainey, Robert Blake, Patrick Bowe, Barbara Brennecke, Michael Brennecke, Patricia Brennecke, Gerald Britain, Beliz Brother, Denise Brown, Ellyn L. Brown, Janice Corcoran, Patty Courtright, Judith Cruise, Lynn Eaton, Lynn Eninger, Dick Farrell, Naomi Fifield, Mark W. Gardner, Elaine R. Giampietro, Esther Greene, Galen Gregory, Noralyn Harlow, June Harris, Lee Anne Hartley, Sabrina Herzog, Ralph Howland, Bill Jackson, Kim Jackson, Peta Jackson, Lois B. Jacobs, M. R. Johnson, Danny Kaplan, Susan Leclerc, Susannah Levine, David Lovejoy, Patty Lyman, Lynn MacAusland, Margaret A. Machulis, Peter Macky, Kent Madin, Sue Maxwell, Lawrence N. Neber, Jonathan Olom, Noralyn Olom, R. Wayne Parker, Ellen Paul, Creighton Peet, Ann Petranoff, Joanna H. Phinney, Carol Plotkin, Catherine M. Preus, Guy Rabut, Keith Ronholm,

Peg Rourke, Jo Ann Schoef, Nancy Schubert, Joan Shafran, Lisa Shattuck, Guerolan Smith, Shari Sobol, Mary Strong, James Swanzy, Tillie Taylor, Lesley Tegenborg, Dottie Thach, Ellen F. Thompson, Tim Thompson, Claudia Velletri, Gerry Vogt, Nancy Watson, Arthur Wells, Susan Welti, Sarah White, Debi Yaglinski, Liz Yoder.

In the case of duplicate recipes, I tended to credit the first student who sent it in. But I would like to list the colleges whose students took time out from their busy schedules to correspond with me and to fill out patiently and return my lengthy questionnaires, and those who sent in recipes but did not sign their names: Barnard College, Boston College, Boston University, University of Bridgeport, University of California (Berkeley), University of California (Irvine), University of California (Los Angeles), University of California (Santa Barbara), University of Colorado, Columbia University, University of Connecticut, Cornell University, Curtis Institute of Music (Philadelphia), University of Delaware, University of Denver, Duke University, George Washington University, Goddard College, Hobart College, Indiana University, Johns Hopkins University, University of Louisville, University of Maine, University of Maryland, Massachusetts Institute of Technology, University of Miami, University of Michigan, Middlebury College, Mills College, University of Minnesota, Nasson College, New England Conservatory of Music, University of New Hampshire, University of New Mexico, New York University, University of North Carolina (Chapel Hill), University of Northern Colorado, Northwestern University, Peabody Conservatory of Music (Baltimore),

ACKNOWLEDGMENTS

University of Pittsburgh, Prescott College, Rice University, Smith College, School of the Museum of Fine Arts (Boston), Syracuse University, University of Texas, Texas Christian University, Tulane University, Union College (Schenectady), Vassar College, University of Vermont, University of Virginia, Williams College, William Smith College, Yale University.

In addition, this book would never have gotten out of the kitchen without the help of Lynn Eaton and Barbara Ann Homan who tested so many of the recipes . . . often making a dish several times in order to work out the quantities and proportions when they were not given in the original recipe.

And finally, I would like to express my gratitude and appreciation to all the students throughout the country whose warm response, enthusiasm, advice, and suggestions made writing this book such a pleasure.

CONTENTS

Introduction   xi
How to Eat Better for Less Money   3
Coming to Terms   14
Cooking Hints   29
A Table of Substitutions   39
Herbs, Seeds, and Spices   43
Granola   55
Breads   62
Soup   74
Eggs   85
Ground Beef   102
Beef   122
Veal   128
Lamb   138
Chicken and Other Poultry   152
Fish   169
Vegetables   178
Rice and Pasta   201
Salads   214
Sauces, Gravies, and Salad Dressings   223
Desserts   230
Things to Eat When You Have to
Stay Up All Night Studying   243
Food for Friends and Other Guests   254
Index   267

To My Mother

INTRODUCTION

The first edition of *The College Cookbook,* which I wrote four years ago, was based on my experiences with my college-age sons and their friends. Through them I had found that the stereotype of the college student who lived on french fries, Cokes, and pizzas was so firmly entrenched that no one had ever bothered to find out what the true picture was. In visiting and talking with students at their colleges, I discovered a culinary sophistication that surpassed that of many of my adult friends. The fact was that many students were cooking food nutritionally and deliciously superior to that of their parents. Their parents thought so, too, and I frequently heard comments such as "Jim does a lot of the cooking when he's home—he's better than I am!" I started collecting recipes from students throughout the country, and the first *College Cookbook* was the result.

At that time I found that, in general, students cooked "from scratch." They did not buy TV dinners or packaged meals and were way ahead of my generation in their knowledge and acceptance of natural foods. Today, going back to the campuses to do research for this book, I have found that this is still true—in fact more so. Student cooking on and off campus has become even more widespread and the students themselves more knowledgeable.

Some of the trends I had observed, such as men as well as women taking a deep and active interest in preparing their own food, have accelerated rather than diminished, and men still seem to develop original recipes more frequently than women. In addition, I have found that men are much more aware of washing-up as a chore and are constantly devising shortcuts for keeping the kitchen neat and orderly as they work; sometimes they even give instructions to this effect in their recipes. Women, on the other hand, seem to be more resigned to a mess after a meal and make little or no effort to minimize it.

There has been one noticeable change since the first edition. With skyrocketing tuition costs and the need to economize wherever possible, student cooking off and on campus has become so common that colleges themselves have become aware of it. In most cases they have bowed to the inevitable to the point of actually encouraging it. Meal plans are offered in a more flexible way so that a student has a choice of cooking in or eating out in the college cafeteria at his or her own convenience. Most colleges routinely provide kitchens for student use in the dorms. As a result, dinner parties are now an accepted form of entertainment among informal student groups (sometimes on a regular weekly basis, with houses alternating as hosts), and the menus on these occasions are eye-openers for those who would expect them to be the equivalent of fast-food meals. All of this has, however, created problems for college administrators, since the number of students who turn up for any given meal is now completely unpredictable; instead of captive diners, they are confronted with students who may elect to prepare their own dinner if they don't like, or can't afford, the college's menu for that night.

Although much college food is still poor to the point of being practically inedible, many schools have tried to solve the cafeteria attendance problem by providing meals more to the students' tastes. Yale and Bennington, for instance, try hard to provide acceptable fare, including yogurt, bean sprouts, and make-your-own salads, as well as to emphasize quality in their raw ingredients. Since almost all college food is provided by food services, there is really not much excuse for poor college food—food services offer excellent as well as awful food, and a menu that leans heavily to spaghetti and meatballs or frankfurters and beans deserves the poor attendance it usually gets.

In spite of the facts, food editors in leading newspapers and magazines continue to publish articles deploring the food habits of the young and viewing with considerable amazement any personal experiences they have with gourmet student cooks. I only wish they would take a short tour of their local colleges and see for themselves the revolution that has taken place. Student-prepared fare is good, wholesome, and interesting. I, personally, would rather eat a dinner prepared by some of my student friends than dine elaborately and expensively in an haute cuisine restaurant. I would be sure everything was fresh, prepared from scratch, as free as possible from additives, and cooked with interest and enthusiasm. I might be startled by a new flavor or an unfamiliar ingredient, but the surprise would almost always be a pleasant one.

Student cooks have gone far beyond the standard recipe books and the recipe cards their mothers have contributed from the family clipping file. Free of traditional prejudices, open to new ideas, influenced by world travel, students today like and make for themselves food that is based on many cultures, ethnic groups, and unusual combinations. Mexican, Chinese, Indian, Italian, Hungarian, Spanish, South American, and French are only some of the cuisines that contribute the dishes they prepare routinely. They cherish their own recipes and will argue vehemently as to whether chili should be made with or without tomatoes, or what combination of foods makes the best paella. They read labels carefully and have nothing but scorn for cottage cheese that contains "flavoring," or junk foods richer in additives than in nutrients. My own cupboard contents have changed drastically over the years since my sons did a bit of consciousness-raising on this subject, and I now know better than to buy anything that contains artificial coloring—at least, if I am aware of it. Students know, also, about the dangers of nitrates and nitrites, and their consumption of hot dogs and bacon has dropped accordingly.

With all of this they are not health food nuts; they strike a remarkably happy balance. They do not blindly accept the merchandise in health food stores—in fact, they consider many of these stores a rip-off and will not buy in them. When they enter the adult world, they will bring with them consumer awareness, a pleasure in their own domestic skills, and a respect for their bodies and what they fuel them with; I only hope they stick to their convictions.

I have very much enjoyed doing this book and working with students around the country. My only regret is that I have had to omit hundreds of fine recipes sent me because there was simply not enough space for them all. I hope you like the ones I have included. Remember, I rely on the feedback I get from my readers to tell me where I have succeeded and where I have gone wrong. If you especially like a recipe and want more like it, let me know; if you don't like a recipe or have a suggestion for improving it, tell me about it. This is your book for your use, and I would like it to reflect your tastes and needs; I particularly would like it to include your favorite recipes so that—through the printed word—they can be shared with other students with the same problems and life-styles.

In closing, I would like to thank you all for your warm reception of my first book which has made this revised edition possible. I hope you like this new version as well as you did the first. If you have any questions or care to write me about your own way of doing things, I would very much like to hear from you.

Geri Harrington
Merwin Lane
Wilton, Connecticut

THE COLLEGE COOKBOOK

HOW TO EAT BETTER FOR LESS MONEY

In a time of rising prices, shopping economically requires fast footwork because the rules change as fast as you learn them. However, there are still some things you can do to get the most for your food money.

If you are *doing your own cooking,* you have already taken the first, and most important, step in eating better for less. You can afford to eat steak at home for possibly less than you would pay for hamburger in a restaurant. And you know it's steak . . . not hamburger made out of what might be a dubious cut of meat.

But to get the most value out of your own cooking, you have to learn how to cook. Generally speaking, *the most expensive things are the easiest to cook.* Cheaper . . . equally delicious foods . . . take a little more skill. Learning to cook is a cumulative process; the more you know, the easier it is to learn more. Master the basics and you won't have any trouble with more complicated recipes. The important thing is to understand what and why you are doing things. Many people follow recipes blindly all their lives and couldn't improvise if survival depended on it. Don't cook like that. Learn how to make soup, stew, a casserole, etc., in a general sort of way and then you can improvise to suit your budget or what happens to be on hand.

Next to eating out, the most expensive thing you can do is to use so-called "convenience" foods. The more that's been done to a food, the more it costs and the less good it is for you. Frozen TV dinners are a perfect example. They are handy and if you eat two of them, you feel full. But a little planning will enable you to have homemade, easy-to-heat-up casseroles in your own refrigerator . . . and they won't contain preservatives and all sorts of artificial "flavor enhancers" and other junk. If you buy frozen vegetables, don't get the ones with built-in sauces or seasonings. You pay a tremendous price for those extras, and you can add them yourself in a minute at little cost. Sauces are simple to make once you get over thinking you can't cook them, and mixed vegetables are no harder to fix from scratch than all of one kind. If you want an example of how much so-called convenience foods are costing you, compare the price of a can of cooked rice with the price of a box of rice . . . and figure out your cost per serving. To save that money all you have to do is wait for the rice to cook . . . you don't even have to watch it or pay any attention to it while it's cooking.

Another way to save money is to *buy the week's specials.* If you don't like what one market is featuring, maybe another nearby has something else. It's possible to save as much as forty to fifty cents a pound on meat if you buy it on "special." It also adds interest to eating. I didn't buy lamb for six weeks this summer because it never went on "special." When I finally did, I bought a leg and we enjoyed it extra-specially because we hadn't had it for so long and thought of it as a real treat.

There is one thing to beware of in buying bargains. The supermarkets know you are looking for specials, so they try to make regularly priced items look special by displaying them as if they were. *If an item is featured, make sure it is actually priced lower than usual.* This means knowing your prices, but if you shop regularly and don't have much money to spend, you will automatically remember what most of your purchases cost. Take a minute to think back to what you paid for it last time and don't touch if it is not a bargain no matter how large a stack of cans they may have pyramided to entice you. Of course, you can't buy *just* bargains . . . but even staples like sugar and hamburger go up and down in price. So do the best you can to buy when things are temporarily lower. Just keep in mind that not all featured items are bargains.

Don't buy dented cans even if they are a bargain. Your doctor bills may more than make up the difference in price.

Don't buy vegetables that look downright old or you will be cheating yourself of the vitamins and minerals you should be getting. But *late Saturday afternoon may offer mark-downs* in fresh produce which won't keep over the weekend. *Slightly* tired lettuce, etc., may still be good to eat. Slightly browned mushrooms are often a very good buy.

Whenever possible, *buy in a market where you can select your own fruits and vegetables* instead of buying them bagged or in a tray. Some supermarkets package lemons with a few fresh and a few on the old side. If you pick them out individually, you can pick out only top quality. This is true of grapes, cherries, etc., too. But if you do buy oranges by the bag (sometimes the cheapest way), look at all the oranges through the plastic to make sure none are spoiled. You can return the spoiled ones and get good fruit in exchange, but that takes a lot of time. If a head of lettuce or escarole has been trimmed so that the dark outer leaves are gone and you can see whitish yellow on the bottom of the outside leaves, that head has been trimmed down because it's old. Not only are you losing the outer dark green leaves which contain the most nutrients, you are buying older greens they had to trim to sell. Let someone else buy them.

Always smell boxes of strawberries before you buy them. If they are fragrant and strawberry-like, and the berries look plump and perfect through all the slits in the sides of the box, they are good berries. If they have a slightly rotten smell, or no smell at all, or have a lot of mashed berries showing on the sides, get something else that day. If even one berry is moldy, pass up that box.

Buy fruits and vegetables in season. When asparagus first comes on the market, it is a luxury. Two weeks later, you can afford to make a meal of it. The same with fruits. So have a little patience. Things in season will not only be cheaper, they will taste better . . . and the pleasure of anticipation will add to your enjoyment when you finally eat them.

If you eat much meat, it is the most expensive part of your food budget, so it's worth learning to buy it wisely. *Get to know what a good piece of meat looks like.* Meat that looks dried out or off-color can easily be recognized even by someone inexperienced. Usually in a supermarket fresh packages of meat and old packages are in the case at the same time. Look around and see if you can spot one of each. The fresh meat will generally look much more attractive than the old meat; once you have seen the difference, you won't be stuck with old meat. Sometimes you can decipher the store's dating code by watching the clerk replenish the cases. Notice the packages she is putting down and compare them with the ones already in the case. You will soon figure out the code . . . it's never very complicated.

If you're on a tight budget, *Don't feel there's nothing between sirloin steak and hamburger.* There are bone-in chuck steaks which cost about the same price as hamburger and make great broiled steaks. Get the cut nearest the rib rather than toward the neck. If it seems tough the first time you try it, marinate it next time and you will be very happy with it. It also provides the basis for lots of dishes like pepper steak which taste great, are a real change from broiled meat, and stretch a pound of meat to feed eight people (with rice, vegetables, etc.). A friendly butcher will answer questions honestly and teach you about the various cuts of meat. Or get a book out of the library and learn one cut at a time. A couple of weeks of this will save you a small fortune the rest of your life and make eating much more interesting. Who would want to live on just broiled steak, broiled chicken, and hamburgers, even if they could afford it?

Whenever possible, shop in a good part of town. Surveys have shown that inner-city markets actually charge more. Another advantage of shopping in a good section is that the overall quality of the food will be more closely controlled. Customers are fussier and won't hesitate to make a commotion if something is unsatisfactory. Also, cheaper cuts of meat are not so much in demand, so they are usually priced somewhat lower than in poor neighborhoods where everyone wants them. Supermarkets usually charge less than independent butchers for things like kidneys, brains, chicken livers, etc. so keep an eye out for them and buy them when you see them (rather than make up your mind ahead of time that that is what you are going to have for dinner).

When it comes to brands of canned goods, *often the store's own brands are your best buy*. They may even be national brands packed under the store's label, in which case, you get a bargain by paying less for exactly the same quality. Stores usually have two grades which they pack under two different names. Check them out by buying one of each and see what you're paying more for. Sometimes it is worth it, sometimes it is not. I find that canned tomatoes vary a great deal in flavor and usually it's worth buying the market's own top grade. In frozen foods, you have the same choice between name brands and store brands. Only experimenting will tell you about quality. However, sometimes the same frozen foods will vary from store to store of the same chain. This is because so much depends on how the food is kept; not all store managers are equally careful. Find a clean, well-managed supermarket and you will have more confidence in what you buy there.

You will save the most on your food bill by *joining or forming a cooperative*. Many groups of students on the West Coast have done this. They buy direct from the farmers at wholesale prices. If you cannot do this, sometimes you can make an arrangement with an independent grocer to give you special prices on the items you use in quantity and could buy by the case. Case-lot prices make sense if you can buy for a large enough group and have the room to store that quantity. However, this is not feasible for most students.

Learn to read labels. They don't give you nearly as much information as they should, but at least learn what you can from them. The first thing to know is that labels are required by law to *have their contents listed in order of quantity;* the ingredient there is most of is listed first, etc. So a can that lists water as its first ingredient contains more water than anything else. If it lists "water, cereal, kidney beans, meat" in that order, you can figure you're not getting much meat. This can be a real give-away as to the contents of a can, so always take the trouble to read it. Sometimes if you are wondering which of two brands to buy, the cheaper brand will show by its list of contents that it isn't as good a buy as the more expensive one. Anyway, always look.

The United States Government specifies standards for certain terms and this is protection for you *if you know what the terms mean.* ' "fruit juice" contains all real fruit juice; whereas "Nectar" or "punch" may be mostly water and sugar with artificial coloring. "Luncheon meat" has more meat than "meat loaf," which is allowed to have more cereal as filler. Meat spreads may be delicious but they contain only about half meat . . . make your own very cheaply with a blender and some spices and know what you're eating. Natural cheese is hard to find but it's a much better buy than process cheese, which contains much more moisture, less milk fat, and is sometimes loaded with chemicals. "Cheese food" may be only 20 per cent cheese and 80 per cent filler, vegetable gum, etc. Make your own chili. You can load it with beans and still get more meat than you would in a can.

Unfortunately, some foods—like ice cream and mayonnaise—don't have to tell you what is in them. They can have artificial coloring, artificial flavoring, or preservatives galore without a word about it on the package. Fortunately, some brands are now making a point of their purity, so *try to buy the brand that seems to care the most about the consumer.* Watch out when you buy yogurt. If the package lists anything unfamiliar as an ingredient, why buy it? Everything needed to make yogurt properly is something you would recognize as a normal ingredient. You will pay more for the real thing but anything else isn't worth eating. Same way with cottage cheese. It should be very fresh and not contain preservatives to extend its "shelf life" for three months or more. I'll never understand why anyone would need to add "artificial flavoring" to properly made cottage cheese. I won't buy cottage cheese if it has anything extra in it.

You would think you would be safe from additives when you buy raw meat. Unfortunately, this is not always true. For instance, smoked hams for baking are often labeled "water added." This means, aside from anything else, that *you are paying baked-ham prices for water . . . sometimes quite a lot of water.*

The meat will seem cheap if you just compare the price per pound to other hams, but it may be more expensive compared to what you are getting; it won't taste as good either. For the same reason, don't buy frozen turkeys with "butter" or any other fat added. You're paying extra for something you don't want and don't need. A good turkey is the easiest thing in the world to cook; it doesn't have to be doctored up for you.

It is usually considered good practice to buy the largest-size package you have room to store. But larger packages are *not always* cheaper than the smaller ones. In fact, sometimes you pay proportionately more for the larger package. *So check before you buy.* For some reason this happens most often with detergents and things like that. It never seems to happen with tea, sugar, etc. However, packaging does make a difference in cost. Spices often come in both plain and fancy packages with a big difference in price for the same contents. Raw sugar, for instance, will usually be cheaper packed in a bag than in a box. In one store the boxed raw sugar was exactly double the price of the identical sugar in the bag.

How you intend using food should be a consideration in buying it. Solid-pack tuna may be desirable for a fancy salad plate, but chunk tuna would save time and money when making a casserole or a sandwich filling. Sliced canned peaches are a better buy than peach halves because they contain more fruit and less syrup. Don't buy a fancy pack unless you have a reason.

Snacks can be a waste of time, money, and nutrition if you eat what is commonly sold as snacks. Fruit and raw vegetables, nuts and seeds, natural juices, etc., make the best and most inexpensive snacks. When preparing vegetables for cooking (carrots, etc.), take an extra minute to make a few carrot sticks, keep out a few flowerets of cauliflower, etc., and use for snacks or in tomorrow's salad. Potato chips and all other deep-fat fried nibbles don't do a thing for you . . . and I notice that most of you said you won't have a thing to do with them. Of course, once in a while, you may eat something thoroughly useless just for fun. But at least know what you're paying a pound for it . . . you might prefer lobster instead!

Some of you buy in health-food stores in an effort to get better food, but as one student puts it, "Health food stores are a rip-off." Well, not all of them are, *but don't buy trustingly in them just because they sell "health foods."* Many of the same items they carry can be found at a more reasonable price in the supermarket; and you can't always be sure vegetables are organic unless you have grown them yourself. So while health food stores may be fun to shop in and sometimes have better products, shop there just as carefully as you would anywhere else.

If this makes shopping sound like a chore, it is. But it is fun, too; and when you realize how much you can save by buying food knowledgeably, and how well you can eat for much less than you thought, it's certainly worth it. Also, it's only hard in the beginning; after a while, it gets to be second nature and doesn't take much longer than just stuffing the shopping cart heedlessly.

The best pots and pans you can buy are your best buy. Good, heavy, well-made pots will last longer and cook more evenly. If you have trouble with everything sticking or burning, maybe your pots are too thin. Start out with just a few, but get good ones.

Take proper care of your equipment. Don't take a pot off the stove and put it in the sink, and don't put cold water in it when it's very hot. Give it a few minutes to cool, then fill with hot water and detergent and let it soak while you eat.

Cast-iron pots should never be really washed . . . just wiped clean with paper toweling. But be sure to follow manufacturer's directions for "seasoning" before using.

Never scour stainless steel. The scouring pad will make thousands of tiny scratches and the next time you cook, your food will stick.

For some reason students seem to gravitate toward enamel pots. They seem cheap . . . but if they are, don't buy them. A good enamel pot is very expensive. The cheap ones are either not real enamel or have a very thin layer of enamel and will chip and burn and not last at all. They also won't cook properly. If all you're going to do is boil water, they're easy to clean. But anything else you use them for is liable to give you trouble unless you have very good quality.

COMING TO TERMS

Cooking terms are a shortcut both in writing and in following recipes. For instance, if a recipe says "cream butter," you can read it faster and follow it more quickly if you know what "cream" means. If you don't know the meaning of a term, look it up the first couple of times . . . after that you will know just what to do. These are terms you asked for definitions of or which you said you had trouble with when you were first learning to cook.

BAKE—To cook in an oven or similar enclosed space by dry heat. Obviously a clambake is not cooked in a conventional oven, but one is created by the sand, rocks, etc. Also there are devices which you can use on a top burner to bake small things like potatoes, muffins, etc. These are sold in hardware stores and are helpful if all the equipment you have is a two-burner hot plate and you are crazy about baked potatoes.

BARBECUE—Anything cooked under a broiler with a barbecue sauce brushed on is said to be barbecued. Originally it was only applied to food cooked slowly over a turning spit, or on a grill over charcoal. It's not very important as a description of a method of cooking but it's colorful in describing your dish. Barbecued spare ribs sound much tastier somehow than broiled spare ribs.

BASTE—To moisten food while cooking. Spooning pan juices over roasting turkey is basting. So is brushing on barbecue sauce while cooking spare ribs. The idea is simply to keep the outside of whatever you are cooking from drying out. It also adds the flavor of your basting liquid and usually helps in browning the food. If you use plastic cooking bags, they are supposed to do the basting for you. I find them good for veal roasts, which otherwise have a tendency to dry out.

BATTER—You won't need to know about this unless you make pancakes or waffles from scratch, or certain fried foods. Batter is flour plus a liquid like milk or water, sometimes eggs too, mixed all together to a consistency which can be poured or dropped from a spoon.

BEAT—You can beat with a spoon, fork, wire whisk, etc. What you are trying to do is add air to a mixture and get all the ingredients evenly mixed. Use rapid motions and get into all parts of the bowl, going down toward the bottom and lifting up to the top each time, with a circular motion.

BLANCH—The confusion a lot of you find in this term is because it applies to three different things:

1. Mostly it means to cook something in boiling water for a very short time . . . not enough to cook it through but merely to soften it a little. In making stuffed cabbage, you blanch the cabbage leaves to soften them so they will bend without breaking when you roll them around the filling.

2. It also means the trick of dipping fruits and some vegetables in boiling water so you can peel them easily. If you need to peel tomatoes, for example, dip them in boiling water; the skin will come off easily, leaving a nice, neat peeled tomato. (If it doesn't, pop it back into the boiling water and leave a minute longer.)

3. The third meaning is almost the same only you dip shelled nuts into boiling water to get the outer skin off.

It's no use trying to tell you how long to keep anything in boiling water (obviously cabbage leaves will take longer to "blanch" than tomatoes) but trial and error works fine . . . you won't spoil anything if you leave it in the water a little too long. Just don't throw out the boiling water until you are sure you are finished with it.

BLEND—To mix two or more ingredients together so that they are evenly distributed throughout the mixture. Sometimes you do this by just stirring, sometimes by beating or folding. It all depends on what is being combined.

BOIL—This term is simple but not very accurate. You need to know the difference between a racing boil, slow boil, and simmer.

Racing Boil—Boiling over high heat so water is bubbling as fast as it can. This is important when cooking spaghetti or adding something to the water which should not stop the water boiling. It is very bad for cooking meat. As one student said in a recipe for stew:

> Meat fast boiled
> Is meat half spoiled.

Slow Boil—Bubbles break the surface in a regular sort of pattern and look like what you think of as boiling. A slow boil does not churn the food around madly. Most vegetables should be boiled this way . . . steadily but not frantically.

Simmer—The slowest boil of all. It means the bubbles rise and break just under the surface so that the water continually ripples. It is the only way to cook something long and slowly so as to bring out the most flavor. Stews, casseroles, and all other long-cooking dishes . . . whether top-of-the-stove or oven-cooked dishes . . . should be cooked this way. Don't cook it with a lower heat than this . . . it should never *stop* simmering . . . but not higher either. You will have to keep an eye on it in the beginning to be sure it is going to keep simmering, but then you can forget about it until it is done.

BRAISE—Even experienced cooks seem to find this a confusing term. I think that is because it is really two steps:

1. Brown the food in a small amount of fat or cooking oil.

2. Cook slowly (simmer) in a small amount of liquid in a flat pan with a good tight cover.

You first brown your meat on all sides, then add some liquid (soy sauce, wine, etc.), cover, and continue cooking until tender. This is great for the inexpensive but flavorful cuts of meat which are too tough for broiling or sautéing. The trick is to use only a small amount of liquid . . . if you use too much you will boil, not braise. Check every so often and add a little more liquid (even water), if necessary. Some things, like tomatoes or zucchini, are watery and add to the liquid you have put in the pan, so until you are experienced, start out with a minimum and increase it when you have simmered the dish for twenty minutes or so. You want to end up with enough liquid for a couple of spoonfuls of gravy or sauce. You may remove the cooked food a few minutes before serving, keep it hot, and thicken the liquid in the pan with flour or cornstarch.

BREAD—To coat with cracker or bread crumbs. Sometimes the food is dipped in milk or beaten egg first.

BROIL—To cook under the broiler unit in your oven or over a fire directly (not in a frying pan). If you cook in a frying pan without fat (or just enough fat to keep the food from sticking), it is called "pan broil" and has a similar effect in terms of taste. *Grill* is the same as *broil.*

BUTTER—To rub a pan or grill with butter or fat so food will not stick to it; it will be easier to clean. Good to do with baking dishes when making macaroni casseroles, etc. An easy way to do it is to put the butter or oil in the pan and rub it around with a piece of wax paper.

CHOP—Cutting things up has an effect on how long you have to cook them. So while chopping is a general term for cutting things into pieces, there are more specific terms which tell you how large the pieces are supposed to be.

Mince—To chop food as finely as possible, short of grinding. Usually done with garlic, onion, etc., when you want it to vanish into the sauce.

Dice—Pieces less than ½" square but not smaller than ¼".

Cube—Pieces ½" to 1" square.

Chunks—Large cubes, about 1½" to 2" square.

Most recipes will specify as above, some will actually say "cut meat in ¾" cubes." With vegetables the terms are usually more general because size isn't as crucial (unless they are shredded or grated).

CLARIFY—Another term with more than one meaning:

To Clarify Stock—Add egg white, egg shells, or raw hamburger and simmer uncovered for 15–20 minutes. Then strain. This will give you a clear broth.

To Clarify Butter—Melt and heat until foamy. Spoon off the foam and carefully pour the clear butter into a container, being careful not to include the white solids in the bottom. The reason for this is that clarified butter is butter without the milk solids. It can be heated to a much higher temperature without burning and is, therefore, better for sautéing than regular butter. I keep a small cup of it in the refrigerator to use whenever I want to fry in butter. It keeps almost indefinitely.

CREAM—To soften butter or shortening by pressing it against the side of a bowl, preferably with a wooden spoon, until it is soft and smooth. Sometimes the fat is worked with sugar, as in making a cake. Sometimes it's just handy for making butter soft enough to spread on sandwiches without tearing the bread.

CRISP—Another two-meaning word:

1. When applied to raw vegetables, it means to make crisp by soaking briefly in ice water and refrigerating . . . as carrot strips, celery, etc.

2. When applied to cooking vegetables, it means to get a crisp outer shell on food by heating it in the oven or under the broiler.

Which only goes to prove that you have to use common sense when following a recipe or you will end up with a salad made of oven-fried carrots.

CUT—This is tricky because it sounds obvious:

1. To separate food into pieces by using scissors or a knife.

But the most important meaning is:

2. To combine butter or shortening with dry ingredients by working them with two knives or a pastry blender. The action is basically a cutting action but the purpose is to mix the ingredients evenly and finely. Since, because of the nature of the things you are trying to combine, you can't just stir them, you keep cutting down through the whole mixture until it looks homogeneous. This is important in making dough and there is no shortcut.

DEGLAZE—A lovely term but all it means is getting off the pieces that are stuck on the bottom of a frying pan by adding water or wine or whatever liquid the recipe calls for, and simmering it while you loosen the burned-on bits with a wooden spoon. It takes about a minute to do, is the easiest way to clean a stuck-on pan, and also adds an incredible amount of flavor to your sauce or gravy.

DEGREASE—This is easy too. It means to remove fat from the surface of liquids. There are lots of ways to do it. The best way is to cool the dish until the fat solidifies; it will all be on top and you can just pick it off.

Or you can drop in a couple of ice cubes. The fat will congeal on them if you remove them immediately. Or brush a lettuce leaf across the surface; the fat will adhere to it.

You can spoon it off . . . since the fat always floats on top of the liquid you can remove the fat by just skimming the surface. This takes a little time and patience but, like the first method, it saves the fat for later use.

If you don't have time to cool the liquid, I find the spooning method works best, but not everyone does. Sometimes it's more efficient to pour the fat into a custard cup or bowl. You will get some of the broth with it but the fat will be in a thicker layer on top and easier to remove.

DEVIL—To mix something, e.g. hard-boiled egg yolks, etc., with mustard or some other hot seasoning. Very tasty and quick. Sprinkle with a dash of paprika and you have a company dish.

DOT—To put small dabs of butter here and there over the top of food before baking or broiling it. Usually the recipe will tell you about how much butter to start with, but common sense is a good guide. As the dish gets hot, see if there is melted butter all over it; if not, add a few more "dots."

DREDGE—About the same as "bread" except it is usually applied to coating something with flour. Easy to do if you put the flour in a plastic bag and put the pieces of meat in the bag and shake.

DRIPPINGS—Just what it sounds like. The fat and juice that drip out of meat when it is cooking. Always save it for gravies, soups, casseroles, or sauces. Put it in a jar in the refrigerator and label with Scotch Tape so you know what kind of meat it came from (like "bacon drippings," "roast beef drippings").

DUST—To sprinkle flour, sugar, or any appropriate ingredient lightly over the surface of the food.

EGGS, BEATEN—Sometimes recipes will call for eggs beaten in various ways. It is usually important to beat them according to these instructions, so here are the terms:

Lightly Beaten—Beat just enough to blend the yolks and whites.

Well-Beaten—As you continue from the lightly beaten stage, the eggs will become frothy and full of air.

Egg Whites, Very Stiff—Separate the whites from the yolks. A simple way to do this is to break the egg in half over the edge of a custard cup, carefully so that you don't break the yolk. *Whites will not beat if there is even a drop of yolk in them.* Then pass the yolk back and forth from shell half to shell half over the cup, letting the white drip down into the cup. (Some students do it by cradling the egg yolk in their hands and letting the white drip down between their fingers, but this is tricky.)

Let the whites warm to room temperature and beat with a fork, whisk, or eggbeater until they stand up in peaks. The points of the peaks should not droop when the beater is removed. The surface of the whipped whites should not look too dry. Use beaten egg whites right away or they will liquify and you will have to start all over again with new egg whites.

Yolks, Well-Beaten—Separate from the whites as directed above. Then beat until they are thick in consistency and lemon-colored.

FOLD—A much gentler mixing action than any other. A way of combining ingredients when one of them is fragile, like beaten egg whites. If you combine them simply by stirring, the whole mixture will collapse; instead add whatever you are adding by putting the ingredient to be mixed into the egg white (or whipped cream, etc.) on top and then, gently, with a spoon or whip, cutting down and over so that the whole mixture is "folded" over and over until it is well mixed.

FRY—To cook in fat in a pan on top of the stove. If you use no fat or very little, you are "grilling" or "pan-broiling." If you use a little fat, you are sautéing." If you use a lot in a deep pan, you are "deep-fat frying" or "French frying."

The important thing about all frying methods is to get the fat hot enough so that the food will cook quickly, forming a crisp outer crust and absorbing as little fat as possible. Sometimes a recipe, for cooking in a *wok,* for instance, will tell you to get the fat "smoking hot." Usually this is too hot but do it if the recipe says to and you have a good ventilator fan.

If you are cooking with butter, it is hot enough when the foam begins to subside. After that it will brown and then burn and you usually do not want this to happen until after you have your food in and cooking.

With an aluminum pan, heat the pan before putting in the butter or oil. With copper-clad pans, you must put the butter or oil in the cold pan; it damages the pan to heat it empty.

When pan broiling, keep pouring off any excess fat or the food will be greasy. In this sense, bacon is pan-broiled rather than pan-fried.

GRATIN or GRATINÉED—A term that looks good on menus or sounds elegant if someone wants to know what's for dinner. It means you covered the cooked food (leftovers, etc.) with a sauce, sprinkled grated cheese or buttered crumbs on top, and dotted the whole thing with butter before putting it in the oven to heat up. Sometimes if it hasn't browned enough in the oven heat, you stick it under the broiler for a minute to get nice and brown. It's an easy, inexpensive way to use up almost anything; if you do it a day or two after cooking the original ingredients, no one will think of it as leftovers gussied up.

GRATE—To cut food up into particles on a grater. There are various kinds. A good, efficient, inexpensive one that can be found in 5-&-10's and hardware stores is four-sided, open at top and bottom, grates in varying degrees of fineness (depending on which side you use), and is a breeze to clean. The food drops down inside and is handy to push off the cutting board into the pot or salad bowl or measuring cup.

GRILL—see "Broil."

GRIND—To crush into very small particles or powder with a mortar and pestle or whatever you have that will do the job. Also, to grind meat, like hamburger, etc.

JULIENNE—To cut into thin strips, like matchsticks. This is used especially for potatoes and carrots which are sufficiently hard to cut small and straight without making a mess. The carrots are good raw and the potatoes French-fried.

KNEAD—To make dough elastic by pressing into it with the heel of your hand until it is stretched and smooth. You have to keep lifting it up, folding it over, and pressing down. It's essential to most bread-making and is a curiously satisfying feeling, like working with clay.

LEAVENING—Something which expands, aerates, and raises other ingredients; like yeast, baking powder, etc., in dough.

LYONNAISE—Another fancy term . . . it means you have added chopped onions to a dish. "Potatoes Lyonnaise," for instance.

MARINATE—To let food soak in a seasoned oil and acid (vinegar, lemon juice, etc.) mixture (called a "marinade"), usually three hours to overnight. It seasons and tenderizes and is good for tough cuts of meat which you want to broil (as in shish kabob). It is fun to use in unexpected ways . . . like marinating a leg of lamb overnight before roasting. It means you can use the same cut of meat all week (if it is very cheap that week) and vary the seasonings to create completely different dishes. For instance, Brazilian beef and Chinese pepper steak vary mostly in the seasoning (coffee instead of soy sauce). It works with vegetables too.

MINCE—see "Chop."

PARE—To cut off (with a knife or vegetable parer) any outside covering, like peeling a potato.

POACH—To cook food in gently boiling (simmering) liquid. Generally used for foods that would break up under rougher treatment (fish, eggs, etc.). Sometimes you have to wrap it in parchment or cheesecloth to keep it whole.

PREHEAT—To heat oven, broiler, etc., to cooking temperature before putting in the food to be cooked. Very important. Take it for granted that you should do it unless the recipes specify a cold oven.

PUNCH DOWN—A term you need to know for baking. Actually punch the dough with your fist, flattening it out in that spot. This allows the gas that has been formed by yeast to escape and allows a fresh supply of oxygen to reach the yeast. Do it evenly throughout the mass of dough.

PUREE—To mash into a baby-food-like consistency. A blender is good for this or you can press the soft food through a sieve. Most vegetables have to be cooked before they can be pureed.

REDUCE—A kind of cooking shorthand. You "reduce" the amount of liquid by boiling it down. For instance, one cup boiled down ("reduced") to three tablespoons. Most reducing can be done at a pretty fast boil. If you overdo it and come out with less than you are supposed to, just add the amount of hot water necessary to make up the right amount of liquid. You usually do it to concentrate the flavor.

RENDER—To melt fat into liquid. Use very low heat and take out the solids when you have as much fat as you need or have patience to wait for.

RISE—Another baking term. To let dough that has yeast in it rise in a warm place . . . usually to double its bulk, but follow the recipe.

ROAST—See "Bake." Most cookbooks will tell you not to add water to a roasting pan. I always do because otherwise the fat burns on the bottom of the pan (unless you are cooking something with a lot of fat, like ham, in which case the fat gets too hot and smokes). A little water keeps the fat from burning or smoking and helps make juice or gravy. Don't add much, just enough to cover the bottom of the pan about ½". If it cooks off, add a little more.

There are also two schools of thought about roasting temperatures. One says start the roast at a high temperature to brown and seal the surface and then reduce the heat for the rest of the cooking time. The other sets the oven at the second temperature to start with and cooks it a little longer. There are two advantages to the second method: you don't have to be around to turn the oven down after the first 15 minutes; the roast doesn't shrink so much, so you get more meat for your money. I much prefer this method. The meat browns beautifully either way.

SAUTÉ—see "Fry."

SCALD—A multiple-meaning term like so many others:

1. To heat to just below the boiling point. Very important with milk to avoid that "boiled" taste most people dislike. With milk, heat until tiny bubbles form around the edge of the pot and then take it quickly off. It must be watched while heating because it happens all of a sudden.

2. To dip in boiling water (see "Blanch").

SCALLOP—This is a term that is practically a recipe because it tells you to arrange food in layers in a casserole, pour sauce over it, sprinkle with a little flour or bread or cracker crumbs, dot with butter and bake. An easy tasty way to combine leftovers with a fresh vegetable and make a good dish . . . like cooked ham and sliced raw potatoes and onions.

SHRED—To tear, cut, or grate into long, flat, narrow pieces with a knife, grater or shredder. Shredded things cook faster than chopped because they are thinner, so it is a good way to treat suitable vegetables. Just shred them, toss lightly in a skillet with hot butter or olive oil, season, and serve. (See recipe for "Shredded Zucchini.")

SIMMER—see "Boil."

SKIM—To remove the top surface, like the fat on chicken soup, the foam on clarified butter, or cream on raw milk.

STEEP—To extract the flavor by soaking in a liquid. What you do when you make tea.

STEW—To cook in simmering liquid until tender. Do not ever let a stew boil faster than simmer or you will lose flavor and tenderness.

STOCK—The liquid in which anything has been cooked, e.g. meat, vegetables, etc. Usually to make a really good stock you start the food in cold water. This extracts most of the nutrients and flavor. Strain when done and throw away the solids. If it happens to be meat, it is too costly to waste, so you eat it . . . but the taste usually needs a boost, like horseradish sauce for boiled beef. To make soup, add whatever meat and vegetables you wish and cook in the hot stock until tender.

TOAST—To crisp and brown by means of dry heat (usually on a flat pan in the oven). If you want to toast bread without an oven or toaster, put a fork through one end and hold over your hot plate, turning as necessary.

TOSS—To mix by lifting the bottom ingredients to the top so that the top falls to the bottom. Should be done with two large spoons or a large spoon and a large fork, without bruising the ingredients . . . as in tossed salad.

WHIP—To beat ingredients that will incorporate air in such a way as to get fluffy . . . like heavy cream, egg whites. Heavy cream should be cold; egg whites room temperature. Beat as fast as possible. If you beat whipped cream too stiff, you will end up with butter.

COOKING HINTS

THINGS NO ONE EVER THINKS
TO TELL YOU

No recipe ever starts at the beginning. It assumes familiarity with certain basic terms, ingredients, and cooking methods. The novice cook has to resign himself to some mistakes; even a very experienced cook will occasionally read a new recipe with a certain degree of puzzlement. There is also the hazard of recipes that have had some essential step or ingredient inadvertently left out. Even *The New York Times* has had to publish corrections and additions to a previous day's recipes. If you find a recipe in a cookbook that doesn't seem to work for you, don't struggle with it too hard. Maybe it wouldn't work for anyone. Of course, I hope that doesn't apply to any of the recipes in this book.

Most recipes do not have to be followed exactly . . . as you will realize when you watch someone at the table add half a shaker of salt to a dish you carefully made with exactly the ½ teaspoon the recipe called for. The recipes that do have to be followed exactly are those for baking bread, cake, etc., or dishes that you want to jell.

Almost any recipe is a jumping-off place for a dozen variations. You can substitute other vegetables, meats, or seasonings. But not indiscriminately, so start out easy. Sometimes just adding or leaving out something as simple as a can of tomatoes will make a completely different dish. To be on the safe side, taste any new dish before you serve it. If it seems lacking, think about combinations you have liked in other dishes. Sometimes all it needs is a flavor boost, and you can save the day by adding a bouillon cube.

When you first start cooking, *keep ingredients simple and as few as possible.* Too many things tend to cancel out one another.

Notice how different methods of cooking affect the taste and texture of food. Broiled chicken and boiled chicken, for instance, are very different. Once you have the difference clearly in mind, you will know instinctively that boiled chicken will make a better salad. This is a great help when you start to improvise.

Seasoning is a personal matter. In testing one of the recipes in this book, I fed the result to four people. One said it needed salt but was fine otherwise; one wanted much more chili; another a little less. I thought it needed a little garlic . . . but then I always do unless it's chocolate fudge. The point is that you have to season lightly until you find out how you want it to taste. Use less rather than more of a seasoning and you won't go far wrong. Too little won't make a dish inedible; too much will.

TO MEASURE ACCURATELY
AND EASILY

Dry Ingredients—Use a metal or plastic measuring cup that fills to the top. Fill cup on level surface and smooth off excess with a knife so top is level. For less than a cup, fill to the correct mark and shake slightly to level.

Liquid Ingredients—Use glass measuring cup that does not fill to the top. Put on flat surface and bend down so your eye is level with the mark. A tall person who doesn't bend down can end up with an eighth of a cup less than he means to.

Solid Ingredients—Fill measuring cup with amount of water equal to the amount of the solid ingredient your recipe calls for. Then add your ingredient until the water measures twice the amount. For example, to measure ½ cup butter: put in ½ cup water; add butter until water reaches 1 cup mark.

Some people have trouble with this but I have never found a better way and would love to know if anyone else has. Sometimes the butter is marked, on the package, in various measures, or you know that so many ounces of something equals so many cups, etc. But sooner or later you are going to have to measure something this way, so you might as well know how.

ALTITUDE ADJUSTMENTS

If you go to the University of Denver or cook in a similarly high altitude, you will have to make certain adjustments in your recipes. Water boils at 212° F. at sea level, at 194° F. at 10,000 feet, so you have to cook stews, soups, or even eggs longer at higher altitudes because boiling water is not so hot as at sea level. There are books with special recipes for high-altitude cooking . . . or you can experiment a little. Your common sense will help you to figure out things like needing more water if you are boiling something longer.

TIMING A RECIPE TO MAKE
EVERYTHING COME OUT
AT THE SAME TIME

In figuring out how long a recipe takes to make, allow plenty of time for preparation. A recipe that says "bake diced carrots and sliced potatoes ½ hour" sounds clear enough. But you have to get the carrots and potatoes out of the vegetable bin, wash them, peel them, and dice them. Then you have to grease the casserole, heat the oven if you forgot to turn it on before you went for the vegetables, and put everything together. By the time you've done everything, the recipe will take a lot more than half an hour. At least in the beginning.

I always used to put spaghetti on the table twenty minutes later than I meant to because I didn't allow for the time it took to get the spaghetti pot out of the back of the cupboard and bring that huge pot of water to a boil. To partially solve this problem, always turn your oven on to preheat before you do almost anything else. Or put water up to boil. If it boils before you need it, take it off the burner; it will still come to a boil more quickly when you are ready for it.

Next, prepare *all* your ingredients to the cooking stage . . . dice, blanch, salt, measure, etc. . . . so that everything is ready to cook, and arranged on little squares of wax paper or in small bowls. Allow plenty of time for browning things. It doesn't matter if browned food cools a little; anyhow you can always keep it hot in a 200° F. oven on a piece of foil. If you need rice, plan to have it ready a little ahead of time. It will become drier and be much better if it cools off just a little.

I also find that a recipe that might be a little tricky or confusing is best tackled with the phone off the hook.

USING AN OVEN

If you have an oven with a thermostat that works, you don't have a problem. The following chart will tell you what recipes mean when they say "in a slow oven," etc.:

very slow oven	250–275° F.
slow oven	300–325
moderate oven	350–375
hot oven	400–450
very hot oven	475 and up

Check out an oven you are using for the first time. Buy an inexpensive portable oven thermometer in any hardware store and set it on the middle oven shelf. Then turn your oven on, setting the thermostat to 350° F. When the light goes off, quickly check the reading on the portable thermometer. It should read 350° F. If it does not, make a note of the discrepancy and adjust your oven setting accordingly whenever you cook in it. Many perfectly good ovens are about 50° F. off their thermostat settings. If your oven is temperamental, use a portable thermometer regularly instead of relying on the thermostat.

Always use a meat thermometer for roasts . . . except poultry. Regardless of whether your oven works or not, insert a meat thermometer into the center of the raw roast; be careful not to touch bone or get the point into a fatty part. The thermometer has a gauge which tells you when the meat is done. Since roasts vary in cooking time due to size, shape, how cold they are to start with, etc., this is your only reliable guide. It will get your meat just as rare or as well-done as you like it every time.

CHEESE

There are thousands of cheeses but they group into three basic categories: soft, semi-hard, and hard. Cream and cottage cheese are soft; münster is semi-hard; cheddar, Swiss, and all grating cheeses are hard.

Soft cheese spoils quickly but hard cheese will keep for ages if tightly wrapped and put in the refrigerator. If hard cheese gets moldy, it doesn't spoil it. Just cut off the actual mold and eat the rest. If it's gotten too dried out, just grate it and sprinkle over something.

Cheeses which depend on molds for their flavor (Roquefort, blue, Stilton) can still get *too* moldy. Examine these cheeses before you buy them; get to know which have reached just the right degree of mold . . . compare the ones in back of the case with the ones in front. Since they are among the more expensive cheeses, they may sit on the store shelf longer than they should. A good dairy department manager in a supermarket automatically puts the older cheeses in front; sometimes a comparison of the front and back of the case cheese packages is very educational. Overmoldy cheeses won't hurt you but they won't taste very good either.

Cheeses are a very valuable food; they contain all the nutrients of milk (except that cream cheese is lower in protein) and are a comparatively inexpensive source of good quality protein. For this reason you should add cheese to your vegetable dishes often . . . especially if you are a vegetarian. A broiled tomato with a sprinkling of grated cheese or a thin slice of mozzarella is immensely better nutritionally than just plain tomato. Cheese doesn't take kindly to very high temperatures. It will melt better if you don't let it get *too* hot.

HEAVY CREAM

Heavy cream will whip better if it is still sweet but not too fresh. A little salt or sugar will help it hold its shape.

CHOCOLATE

Not all chocolate is sweet. If it is called "cooking chocolate," it is unsweetened or "bitter" chocolate. Make sure you buy the type the recipe calls for. In melting milk chocolate, melt in coffee instead of in water and you will have mocha.

To Grate Chocolate. Chill thoroughly first.

To Melt "Cooking Chocolate." Put in the top

of a double boiler and melt over hot but *not boil-ing* water. If the water is boiling, the steam may condense on the cover and drip back into the pan of chocolate. Even a little water will spoil cooking chocolate.

EGGS

Eggs are comparatively delicate and should not be cooked with high heat unless you want to make them tough.

Never salt scrambled eggs or fried eggs until you are serving them. Salting them during cooking will toughen them.

Cold eggs separate easiest. Eggs at room temperature whip best.

Dishes, pans, forks, etc., which you have used for mixing, cooking, or eating eggs should be soaked in *cold* water before washing. Hot water will "set" the egg and make it much more difficult to clean off.

Store eggs in the refrigerator large end up. Ideally, they should be covered. The box they come in from the store is a good way to keep them in the refrigerator. If you make a recipe that uses only egg whites, put the yolks, covered with cold water, in a tightly covered jar and store in the refrigerator.

BAKED HAM

Comes two ways; cooked and uncooked. Always ask the butcher which you are buying unless cooking directions are on the package.

Put the ham on your rack fat side up and it will baste itself. Put 1" of water in bottom of pan so fat will not get smoking hot or spatter.

LETTUCE AND OTHER SALAD GREENS

Tear instead of cutting for a tossed salad. Salad greens should always be quite dry or the oil will not cling to them properly.

In adding oil and vinegar to a tossed salad, always add the oil first. Toss to coat all the ingredients; then add vinegar and toss again.

MEAT

To Store. Raw meat should be refrigerated loosely wrapped. Always remove meat from the store's wrapping, put on a dish, and lightly cover with wax paper.

Cooked meat should be cooled, then tightly covered and refrigerated as soon as possible after cooking.

To Broil. Lamb chops, etc., won't curl up when broiling if you slash the fat all around the edge at 1″ intervals. This works with bacon too, but I don't think it's worth the trouble.

Before putting any food in the broiler, turn on the dial setting to "broil" and preheat for 10 minutes. It's a good idea to heat your broiling pan at the same time. (Put a piece of foil in the pan under the rack to catch the fat.) To test for doneness, make a tiny slit in the meat near the bone and look at it. Broiling time varies with the thickness of the cut, the size of the fish or chicken, etc.

Never salt meat before broiling. The salt draws out the juices and makes it dry and tasteless.

Turn broiling meat with tongs, not with a fork. A fork will make holes in the seared surface and the juices will run out.

Pan-broiling works with slices of meat less than 1″ thick. Ideally you should use a skillet you can preheat. After turning, lower the temperature slightly.

Use thick pork chops for baking; thin ones for pan-frying.

OILS FOR COOKING

Butter adds a nice flavor but burns at a comparatively low temperature. However, clarified butter (see cooking terms) will get much hotter before burning.

Peanut, corn, and sesame-seed oils will not burn until they reach a comparatively high temperature.

Safflower oil gets rancid fairly quickly so try to buy it in small quantities.

Olive oil adds the most flavor of the vegetable oils because it is the least refined. Virgin oil is the most flavorful of olive oils because it is not refined at all. The flavor varies depending on whether it is French, Italian, or Spanish, but most of the olive oil you use is Italian; the French is very expensive. The flavor enhances a dish but there are times when you don't want an olive-oil flavor . . . in frying eggs for breakfast, for instance . . . so don't use it indiscriminately. Olive oil should not be stored in the refrigerator; it will solidify.

If you need only a little oil, cut off a piece of fat, instead, from whatever meat you are cooking (pork chops, etc.) and heat it slowly in your frying pan. After a few seconds, rub it over the entire surface with a piece of wax paper. This won't work if you need much fat but it is a money-saver if you need to grease the pan lightly.

If a recipe calls for "melted" butter or shortening, always measure *before* melting.

A TABLE
OF SUBSTITUTIONS

This is a table that will help you in substituting one ingredient for another in a recipe. You will find it handy when you are missing an ingredient called for but think maybe you have something that will do just as well (e.g. dry herbs for fresh herbs); or you may prefer one ingredient to another (rye flour to white flour, for instance). Substitutions are not fool-proof, however. Generally speaking, honey can be substituted for sugar if you adjust the liquid in the recipe—but there are many different kinds of honey and you may want to use more or less depending on the type. In addition, you have to take into account differences in color, texture, and flavor that will occur as you change ingredients. Although it is possible to use cornmeal and white flour interchangeably in some recipes, the resulting finished products will be very different. It's also fun to experiment and discover your own variations; in any case, think of this table as a beginning, not as an infallible guide.

1 fresh garlic clove
½ teaspoon garlic powder

1 teaspoon fresh ginger
½ teaspoon ground ginger

1 tablespoon fresh herbs
½ to 1½ tablespoon dried herbs

1 oz. cooking chocolate
3 tablespoons cocoa plus 1 tablespoon fat

1 cup white sugar
1 cup well-packed brown sugar
2 cups corn syrup and reduce liquid
  in recipe
¾ cup honey and reduce liquid in recipe
1½ cups maple syrup and reduce liquid
  in recipe
1½ cups molasses and reduce liquid in recipe
1½ cups sorghum and reduce liquid in recipe

1 cup all purpose white flour
1 cup unbleached white flour
1 cup rye flour
1 cup wholewheat flour
⅓ cup soybean flour plus ⅔ cup
  all purpose flour
1 cup and 2 tablespoons cake flour
⅞ cup rice flour
1 cup cornmeal

1 cup white rice
1 cup brown rice and allow more liquid and
  longer cooking time

1 cup butter

⅞ cup corn or peanut oil

1 cup margarine

⅞ cup lard plus 1 teaspoon salt (Lard cannot *invariably* be substituted for other fats since its fat content differs somewhat. For frying, etc., it won't cause any problems.)

1 cup fresh milk

½ cup evaporated milk plus ½ cup water

¼ cup dry milk solids plus ¾ cup water

½ cup condensed milk plus ½ cup water and less sugar than the recipe calls for

to make 1 cup sour milk; add 1 tablespoon vinegar or lemon juice to enough milk so that together they make one cup of liquid . . . allow to stand 5 minutes.

1 teaspoon baking powder
(tartrate or phosphate)

⅔ teaspoon double action baking powder

¼ teaspoon baking soda plus

½ teaspoon cream of tartar

¼ teaspoon baking soda plus

⅓ cup molasses

Note: When the recipe calls for baking powder, use *exactly* the one specified. There are three kinds and they act differently. If you use the wrong kind, your recipe may not work.

1 cup yogurt

1 cup buttermilk

1 tablespoon flour (as a thickener)
   ½ tablespoon cornstarch
   2 teaspoons quick cooking tapioca
   ½ tablespoon potato flour
   ½ tablespoon barley flour
   ½ tablespoon arrowroot

Note: All of the above ingredients, if used correctly, will satisfactorily thicken the liquid to which they are added; but they produce different results. For instance, flour makes an opaque liquid (like a standard brown gravy); cornstarch makes a translucent sauce (like Chinese gravies); minute tapioca can always be detected by its tiny clear globules. The only way to become familiar with these different results is to try the thickeners out; then you will know the one best suited to the results you want to achieve with any given recipe.

HERBS, SEEDS, AND SPICES

When I asked students in colleges throughout the country what spices they used in their cooking, I ended up with a list of forty-two different ones. Many answers weren't counted because they said simply "all of them." "We firmly believe," one wrote, expressing the opinion of many, "that using wines and spices in cooking can make the most inexpensive meats much, much better tasting." Vegetarians, too, used wines and spices generously. Even one of the few students who does not use spices said he used "honey and sea salt only," which somehow seems to open up many flavorsome possibilities. However, you indicated you wanted to know even more about herbs and spices than you already do. You asked, in particular, for information as to what to use with what foods. So I have divided this chapter into two parts:

1. A listing of herbs, spices and seeds most commonly used with some general information about them.

2. A short list of some vegetables and meats and what spices, herbs, and seeds go with them. This is not meant to be used as an inflexible rule, merely as a guide until you know your own mind and can invent your own combinations.

HERE ARE SOME GENERAL HINTS:

• No recipe can really tell you *exactly* how much seasoning to use. Individual tastes vary too much. Even simple seasonings like salt and pepper cannot be pinned down. That is why so many recipes say "salt and pepper to taste." No matter how famous its chef, no restaurant would dare omit the salt and pepper shakers from its tables.

• It is always safer to use too little seasoning than too much. When increasing the amount of seasoning in a recipe, increase a very, very little at a time.

• Some herbs and spices are delicate and lose flavor with prolonged cooking. If the recipe says to add something toward the end of the cooking period, take this seriously. Otherwise you may cook out all the flavor you think you are adding. Once in a while, but very rarely, a spice gets stronger the more you cook it.

• Always taste a dish just before it is done. You can usually correct the seasoning at that point, especially if it is too bland. If you have oversalted, you are in trouble. Try adding two or three potatoes, quartered, and cooking for about 10 or 15 more minutes. Then remove the potatoes . . . if you are lucky, the salt will come out too.

• Buy good-quality herbs and in small amounts. Keep them out of the sun and away from the heat of the stove in air-tight containers. Don't pay for fancy packaging each time . . . invest in good containers and keep refilling them.

• Salts (celery, garlic, etc.) are dried, powdered herbs and spices mixed with common table salt.

Powders (garlic powder, etc.) are not mixed with salt and are, therefore, much more concentrated. I find it easier to use salts because I usually use it without measuring . . . like sprinkling on hamburgers . . . and I don't have to be as careful about how much I use. If you use garlic salt when the recipe calls for fresh garlic, cut down on the amount of salt indicated. (Taste to tell how much.)

● *Bouquet garni* and *fines herbes* are two different combinations of herbs. *Bouquet garni* is generally a bay leaf, some parsley, and thyme. *Fine herbes* are frequently parsley, chives, chervil, and a little tarragon. The combination should be wrapped in a piece of cheescloth, tied securely with a string, and lowered into the liquid of whatever you are cooking. When the dish is done, remove the bag of seasonings. I prefer to have the bits of herbs floating around, but if you want a perfectly clear consommé, for instance, that would not do.

ALLSPICE. Derives its name from the fact that its pungent smell and taste are like nutmeg, cinnamon, and cloves all mixed together. If you like it, use it with almost everything from stew to dessert. Also good with vegetables such as carrots, squash, turnips; and with cooked fruit and puddings. Goes with tomato juice, tomato dishes, all meats and poultry (and soups made with them). Use about ¼ teaspoon to 2 quarts of liquid or to an average casserole.

ANISE. If you think of this as licorice, you won't go far wrong since it is used to give a licorice flavor to cookies and cakes. You can use ¼ to ½ teaspoon in the average recipe (to one cup of liquid or to sprinkle over a salad, for instance). It is interesting mixed with stewed fruit, added to fruit juices, and adds a pleasant flavor to chicken or rice. Cottage cheese and yogurt, too. Don't use it combined with other spices unless you are very sure it will go.

BASIL. This happens to be one of my favorites and I almost never use tomatoes in an Italian recipe without it. To see what a perfect combination that is, try broiled tomatoes (tomatoes cut in half and stuck under a broiler for 10 minutes) both with and without a sprinkling of basil. (I also add a little garlic salt and grated cheese, but I guess that is beside the point.) Anyhow, broiled tomatoes with basil is the simple sort of dish that will give you a reputation as a good cook without any work on your part. Another simple, reputation-making dish is tomatoes sliced thick and arranged on a plate with alternate slices of very thin mozzarella. Drizzle olive oil and vinegar over it, sprinkle with basil and salt, and serve as if you were handing around rubies and pearls. Basil is also good with zucchini, peas, eggplant, and stews. It has a basically delicate flavor and can be used a little more freely than some herbs.

BAY LEAF. This is the old-fashioned herb which is especially traditional for stews. You usually take the large flat leaf out just before serving the cooked dish. One leaf is usually enough. It is good, also, with many sauces and with vegetable soup. It isn't used much, however, with boiled vegetables.

CARAWAY. These are the seeds you find in rye bread. They are great with boiled cabbage or hot sauerkraut, and, if added to the water in which you are boiling shrimp, will cut down on the shrimp smell. Use them fairly freely in cheese dishes, salads, white sauces, and soups; sprinkle over boiled carrots, onions, and turnips. Mixed with softened butter, they make a nice spread for wheat crackers or whole wheat bread topped with cucumbers and sour cream.

CARDAMON. Unless you have a very complete spice shelf, you probably won't have this. Cinnamon will take its place most of the time, or you can use cardamon wherever you would cinnamon. If you want to know exactly what the difference is, mix a little of each with a little sugar and sprinkle on a corner of buttered toast to taste.

CAYENNE. This is colorful and *hot.* It is made from dried, ground chili peppers. Use it whenever you want a bit of excitement; in deviled eggs, guacamole, cheese dishes, broiled chicken, or shrimp. But use it *very* sparingly, especially if you have guests.

CELERY SALT. See "Celery Seed." This is just ground celery seed mixed with table salt.

CELERY SEED. A very useful seed when you don't have fresh celery handy. It isn't celery at all but it tastes as if it were and is great in soups, juices, omelets, stews, and with chicken dishes. Use any place you'd like a touch of celery flavoring and use fairly freely.

CHILI POWDER. A mixture of spices which varies according to the manufacturer. It comes "hot" and "mild," so buy according to your preference. Chili powder gives the characteristic taste to the mixture of kidney beans and ground beef which we call "chili." You can also use it for dips and to sprinkle over broiled meats, add to a marinade, or put in a casserole. Some people like it with tomato and eggplant dishes. You either like it or you don't . . . so go easy if you aren't familiar with the flavor. To make a mild chili hotter, add a little cayenne.

CHIVES. A very mild form of onion that can be easily grown in your kitchen window, handy for chopping up in scrambled eggs. Good also in sauces, soups, and salads, and to mix with cottage cheese. The green color adds eye appeal and the onion taste is subtle and agreeable.

CINNAMON. Almost everyone knows what cinnamon tastes like. It can be used wherever you like it. Apple pie, of course (except *green* apple pie), stewed fruit and, in stick form, for stirring hot cider. Also with carrots and sweet potatoes or winter squash, and in all chocolate dishes. Interesting in cranberry juice and, mixed with sugar, *essential* for cinnamon toast. You can get tired of it, though, so use judgment.

CLOVES. Most people have eaten baked ham studded with cloves and know its delightful fragrance. If you add four whole cloves to two quarts of of chicken broth, you will have a delicious soup. An onion studded with cloves is an easy way to flavor stew. It's good with all ham and pork dishes, with carrots, yams, squash, onions, and many desserts and cooked fruit. Try it in tea.

CURRY POWDER. Some people make their own but most prefer to buy this mixture of spices ready-made. Like chili, curry powders vary considerably from mild to hot and can be very, very hot indeed. What makes it hot is good old cayenne pepper, so add a little if your curry is too mild. If you like curry, add it to a white sauce and pour over any combination of cooked meat, fish, or leftover vegetables to serve on hot rice. Don't use more than ½ to 1 teaspoon for a 6-serving recipe until you find out *how much* you like. It is good in pea soup and is the primary seasoning in mulligatawny soup. A good cheap meal is hot hard-cooked eggs sliced over hot rice with a curried sauce poured over the whole thing.

DILL. This is an herb appreciated more in Scandinavia than here . . . which is too bad. Fresh dill, minced and sprinkled over boiled potatoes (the way you do parsley) adds a Scandinavian flavor and turns an ordinary dish into something special. Dill is good with anything you cook or serve with sour cream (except sweet things or fruit), potato salad, seafood, creamed foods, and, of course, for pickling.

GARLIC. This is my favorite of all herbs, and sooner or later I use it in almost everything except desserts . . . in soups, stews, casseroles, sauces, salads, garlic bread. Not everyone shares my enthusiasm, however, so go easy. Garlic salt in salad won't leave an odor on the breath the way fresh garlic will . . . sometimes that is a consideration. A fresh garlic clove is much better than garlic salt if you have the time to work with it. For just a hint of flavor in a tossed salad, rub it on bread cubes and toss the cubes in the salad with your dressing. Remove cubes before serving salad. Garlic salt is good sprinkled (sparingly) on hamburgers or broiled chicken.

GINGER. A spice that's fun to use unexpectedly because it's almost always pleasant and hard to figure out. Try it in a simple, basic macaroni-and-cheese recipe. Or with hot, buttered carrots or yams. Add it to apple dishes and juices; mix with cream cheese for a spread. If you make a cup of chicken broth, stir in a little ginger. Try it with plain yogurt. This is one spice you can improvise with.

MARJORAM. A gentle relative of oregano. Because it is one of the more aromatic herbs, don't use more than ½ teaspoon to 6 servings. It is very versatile and can be used in just about everything . . . from spreads to stews. Try it where you feel the need of a new taste. Chances are you won't actively dislike it no matter what you cook it with . . . even scrambled eggs.

MINT. Of course you know what mint tastes like. But you might not think to sprinkle it on green peas or carrots (and soups made from these vegetables). Add it to juices, cooked fruit; sprinkle in salads. Make a mint sauce for roast leg of lamb.

NUTMEG. Sweet and fragrant sprinkled over rice pudding; tasty with onions, tomatoes, or green beans. Try it in something unexpected . . . just taste a little on the tip of your finger to see what you're dealing with.

OREGANO. The spice that makes pizzas what they are. It's strong and should be used sparingly. All tomato and most meat dishes like it; so do broccoli, eggplant, dried bean casseroles, eggs. Try ¼ teaspoon to 6 servings. Add to broths for drinking or cooking.

PAPRIKA. So colorful that many dishes call for it just for its decorative quality. It makes broiled chicken look elegant and, of course, is traditionally added in great quantities to Hungarian dishes. If you want to make it hot, add cayenne. A little sprinkled on broiled fish gives it a company look. It is good with cauliflower. If you use just a little, the flavor will not be too obtrusive; if you want to use a lot, and are sure you like the flavor, use it freely.

PARSLEY. An herb which adds vitamins, minerals, color and an invariably pleasing flavor. Add it just before serving, when possible, to get the most nutrients out of it. It can be served whole, with just the stem removed, or minced. Mix it with salads, cottage cheese, all soups and any sauce. Also an easy way to make scrambled eggs look like company fare. Toss with hot, boiled noodles and cottage cheese for a quick, inexpensive, and healthful supper, or stir into sour cream or yogurt with a little lemon juice and you have a good salad dressing. You simply can't go wrong with parsley no matter how much or how little you use.

POPPY SEEDS. An interesting way to add a nutlike flavor to hot, buttered noodles or rice. Good, too, with carrots, summer squash, cabbage, green beans. Mix with cottage cheese or cream cheese. Also used for baking, of course.

ROSEMARY. It smells so good that it was once used (like pine needles) to stuff pillows and scent soap. Don't use too much of it, though. It is almost essential for roast lamb (rub over the surface), good with seafood and baked chicken. I like it in tomato dishes and stews, also. Just use ½ teaspoon for the average recipe for 6.

SAFFRON. This has the dubious honor of being the most expensive of all spices. So naturally, there are imitations to beware of. If you buy a thimbleful (the way it is often sold), be sure it is the real thing. Use very sparingly . . . a little goes a long way. It turns rice a lovely yellow color (for paella, etc.) and adds a pleasant, off-beat flavor to chicken and egg dishes. If all you want is the color, use turmeric instead; it's lots cheaper and has an interesting taste.

SAGE. The very strong and pungent odor that used to come from your grandmother's roasting turkey . . . no self-respecting Colonial stuffing would have been made without it. Use very little—but you can try it with anything from pork to cheese dishes . . . even stuffed cabbage.

SESAME. I think you probably use more sesame seeds than any generation of cooks for centuries. They are best toasted (which gives them a nuttier flavor), and can be added wherever you would use nuts. Sprinkle them on vegetables, mix them with butter or cream cheese, add them to salads, chicken, noodles. To toast, put them in a 350° F. oven for 25 minutes or until they have turned a pale brown color. Be sure they are spread over the pan so that they do not lie one over the other.

TARRAGON. If I had to say what this tastes like, I would say licorice, but there is a subtle difference that makes it good for flavoring vinegar, baked chicken, sauces, Don't use too much of it, but try it with carrots, onions, tomatoes. Capers are traditionally bottled in tarragon vinegar, so when you add them to salads, use the liquid too.

THYME. Start with ¼ teaspoon to a recipe for 6 as this is fairly strong in flavor. It is essential in fish stews; try it also with meat stew, carrots, squash, onions, tomato juice, or mix with cottage or cream cheese to scramble with eggs.

TURMERIC. Basically mustardy in taste. Adds a lovely golden-orange color to sauces or rice. Start with ¼ teaspoon for 6 servings and increase to taste and color desired. Good with chicken dishes and creamed recipes.

SEASONING SUGGESTIONS
(one at a time unless you are *sure*)

Avocado; cayenne, garlic, chili powder

Beans, dried: oregano, parsley

Beans, green: nutmeg, parsley, poppy seeds, sesame seeds

Broccoli: oregano

Cabbage: caraway seeds, poppy seeds, sesame seeds

Carrots: allspice, caraway seeds, cinnamon, cloves, dill, ginger, mint, parsley, poppy seeds, tarragon, thyme

Cauliflower: paprika, parsley, sesame seeds

Cheese: caraway, cayenne, parsley, poppy seeds, sesame seeds, thyme, nutmeg

Cottage cheese: anise, chives, parsley, sesame seeds

Eggplant: basil, chili, garlic, oregano

Eggs: cayenne, celery seed, chives, curry, dill, oregano, parsley, thyme, turmeric

Fish: curry, dill, paprika, parsley, rosemary, thyme, garlic

Ham: cloves

Lamb: curry, garlic, mint, parsley, rosemary

Meats: allspice, chili, curry, garlic

Onions: caraway, cloves, curry, nutmeg, tarragon, thyme

Peas: basil, cloves, mint, parsley

Potatoes: dill, parsley

Poultry: allspice, curry, garlic, ginger, parsley, sesame seeds, anise, cayenne, celery seed, anise, rosemary

Rice: turmeric, saffron, curry, anise, garlic, parsley, poppy seeds, sesame seeds

Squash, winter: allspice, cinnamon, cloves, ginger, thyme

Stews: allspice, basil, bay leaf, cloves, garlic, parsley, oregano, thyme

Tomatoes: allspice, basil, chili, dill, garlic, nutmeg, oregano, parsley, tarragon, thyme

Turnips: allspice, caraway seeds

Yams or sweet potatoes: cinnamon, cloves, ginger

Yogurt: anise, ginger, mint

Zucchini: basil, garlic

This list is meant only to suggest possibilities . . . not to exhaust them. Do not lose sight of the fact that food tastes good in itself . . . too many spices spoil rather than enhance a dish. But the right spice in the right dish is a lovely thing.

GRANOLA

Recipes included and the main ingredients needed

MIKE'S GRANOLA
Oats, wheat flakes, rye flakes, cashews, shredded coconut, raisins, pumpkin seeds, wheat germ, soybeans, almonds, sunflower seeds, oil, honey, vanilla

MINNESOTA MULTI GRANOLA
Quick or old-fashioned oats, coconut, wheat germ, pecans, soybeans, rye flakes, soy flakes, wheat flakes, currants, dried apricots, sesame seeds, honey or brown sugar, oil, vanilla

SUE'S GRANOLA
Old-fashioned oatmeal, almonds, sesame seeds, sunflower seeds, coconut, soy flour, powdered milk, wheat germ, honey, oil, dates

JODI'S GRANOLA
Oats, pecans, almonds, peanuts, maple syrup, safflower oil, currants

DANNY'S GRANOLA
Oatmeal, almonds, sesame seeds, soy flour, powdered milk, wheat germ, oil, honey

Cereal is a good way to start the day. One student wrote, "The best is Irish oatmeal left overnight to cook on the back of an old coal stove, ready to eat in the morning all nutty-tasting and steaming hot. But I have to get up two hours earlier if I want to make it on my hot plate . . . it never seems worth it, so I eat granola instead." So, it seems, does everyone else. And many of you feel very strongly against some breakfast foods . . . as one student put it, "You are what you eat. War should not be waged in human stomachs."

I never meant to have a whole chapter . . . even this mini one . . . on granola, but I received so many recipes for making your own that I thought I would pass on to you the five I liked best. They're all just a little different from one another and you may be able to tell which would be most to your taste just by reading each list of ingredients.

From the School of the Museum of Fine Arts:

Mike's Granola

Really good granola. We make 18 pounds every two weeks—costs about 70¢ a pound but it's much better than other cereals (tastewise and health-wise).
  Preheat oven to 325° F.

2 lbs. oats, rolled
2 lbs. wheat flakes
2 lbs. rye flakes
2 lbs. chopped cashews
2 lbs. shredded coconut
3 lbs. raisins
½ lb. pumpkin seeds, chopped
1 jar wheat germ
1 lb. roasted soybeans, chopped
½ to 1 lb. almonds, chopped
2 lbs. sunflower seeds
corn, soy or safflower oil
honey
vanilla

Mix all dry ingredients, then divide into 11-cup portions. For every 11-cup portion, heat ½ cup corn, soy, or safflower oil plus 1 cup honey and 2 teaspoonfuls vanilla. When heated, mix with each 11-cup portion. Spread on cookie sheet and bake for about 12 minutes, turning over at least every 5 minutes. spread out to dry.

From the University of Minnesota:

Minnesota Multi Granola

We think this recipe is great! For all ages—for both "squares" and "freaks." May be eaten as a cereal with milk, used over ice cream, or just enjoyed as a wholesome snack.
 Preheat oven to 350° F.

6 cups quick or old-fashioned oats, uncooked
2 cups flaked or shredded coconut
1½ cups wheat germ
1½ cups pecans, chopped
1½ cups ground roasted soybeans
1 cup *each;* **rye flakes, soy flakes, wheat flakes,**
1 cup toasted sesame seed
1 cup honey or brown sugar
1½ teaspoons salt
1 cup vegetable oil
1½ teaspoons vanilla
2–3 cups currants and apricots, chopped

Combine dry ingredients in very large bowl. You may want to store half of this amount, as all of it will need two large cookie sheets to bake.
 Add rest of ingredients, except dried fruit. Mix well. Bake for about 30 minutes, turning gently after first 15 minutes. As soon as you remove it from the oven, add the dried fruits and mix well.

From the University of Louisville:

Sue's Granola

Some people use this granola for morning cereal as is. We think it is too rich alone, and use several tablespoonsful plus half a cup or so of Special K with skim milk . . . and find it very good.
Preheat oven to 250° F.

1 cup vegetable oil
1 cup honey
5 cups old-fashioned oatmeal
1 cup almonds, sliced or broken
1 cup sesame seeds
1 cup sunflower seeds
1 cup unsweetened shredded coconut
1 cup soy flour
1 cup powdered milk
1 cup wheat germ
1 cup chopped dates

Mix oil and honey. Mix all other ingredients. Pour oil and honey mixture over other ingredients and stir to combine thoroughly. Toast on flat pan in oven for 30 minutes, or so, stirring every 10 minutes. Cool and pack in plastic bags or canisters and refrigerate or freeze to keep from turning rancid. (If you omit the coconut, it will keep longer.)

From Goddard College:

Jodi's Granola

You can change this slightly if you have a preference for, say, raisins or cashews.
    Preheat oven to 350° F.

8 cups rolled oats
1 cup pecans, chopped
1 cup almonds, chopped
1 cup peanuts, chopped
1 cup maple syrup
1 cup safflower oil
1 cup currants

Sauté oats in small amount of oil in frying pan for 5
minutes, stirring constantly. Place in bowl with all
other ingredients. Mix well. Spread on cookie sheet
and bake until done but not burned . . . about 20
minutes. Keep mixing so bottom doesn't get burned.
The important thing about the ingredients is the
ratio 8 to 1 between the rolled oats and everything
else.

From Prescott College:

Danny's Granola

Preheat oven to 300° F.

5 **cups oatmeal**
1 **cup almonds**
1 **cup sesame seeds**
1 **cup soy flour**
1 **cup non-instant powdered milk**
1 **cup wheat germ**
1 **cup oil**
1 **cup honey**

Combine dry ingredients. Add honey and oil. Spread on cookie sheets. Bake for ½ to 1 hour or until slightly brown.

BREADS

Recipes included and the main ingredients needed

BREAD
  Whole wheat flour, honey, safflower oil, dry yeast

TILLIE TAYLOR'S ZUCCHINI BREAD
  Eggs, sugar, baking powder, zucchini, flour, pecans

CUBAN WATER BREAD VARIATION
  Flour, yeast, sugar

YOGA BANANA BREAD
  Flour, yogurt, bananas, eggs

MY BREAD
  Cracked wheat, dry milk, molasses, honey, oil, yeast, wheat germ, sunflower seeds, rye flour, whole wheat flour

POPOVERS
  Flour, milk, eggs

MOLLY HALL'S BREAD
  Flour, powdered milk, yeast, sugar, shortening

BUTTER DIPS
  Flour, butter, baking powder, milk

HOT CINNAMON PUFFS
  Flour, butter, sugar, egg, baking powder

BROWN BREAD
  Flour, eggs, molasses, shortening, soda, nuts, raisins

If anyone doubts that today's students are serious about cooking, nutrition, and getting back to basics, all they have to do is take a quick survey of how many are baking their own bread. In recognition of this, colleges throughout the country are beginning to offer courses in bread-making. This is the more remarkable in that many of them that are doing so do not particularly encourage their students to live off campus or cook in the dorms. Generally speaking, students who make their own bread do so in a search for a better product. One student wrote, "We bake our own bread and refuse to use bleached white flour, white sugar, or other artificial foods which are pure poison." Not everyone feels that strongly (as you can see from some of the recipes in this chapter), but all report that making bread is one of the most satisfying of activities. A well-baked loaf of bread not only tastes good, it gives the baker a real sense of accomplishment.

Most commercial breads, even those made of comparatively good ingredients, just don't seem to compare with the homemade product. And the better brand-name breads have become so expensive that many people cannot afford to buy them freely.

Since a number of students use basically the same bread recipes, some recipes which I have included may have come from several colleges. In this case, I have simply credited the first college to send it in. Whether or not you've been baking your own bread, try one or two of these really great recipes. As one contributor wrote, "I am enclosing a couple of our bread recipes, simply because they're fantastic."

From the University of California at Los Angeles:

Bread

This is the real thing. You can vary the flour type, sweetening, and oil and add all sorts of things like currants or nuts or cheese if you want.
　　Preheat oven to 350° F.

1. **6　cups lukewarm water**
　　2　packages dry yeast (2 tablespoons)
　　¾　cup honey
　　7–9　cups whole wheat flour

2. **2½　tablespoons salt**
　　½ to 1　cup safflower oil
　　6–8　cups additional whole wheat flour
　　for kneading: 2–3　cups whole wheat flour

Dissolve yeast in water. Stir in honey. Stir in 7–9 cups whole wheat flour until thick batter is formed. Beat well with spoon. Let rise 1 hour.

　　Fold in salt and safflower oil. Fold in more flour until dough comes away from sides of bowl. Knead on floured board, using more flour as needed to keep dough from sticking to board. (Flour your hands for the same reason.) Takes 15–20 minutes. When dough is smooth and satiny, put in warm place, and let rise 50 minutes. Keep out of drafts.

　　Punch down. Let rise again for 40 minutes. Shape into loaves and put in pan. Or just shape into balls and put on cookie sheets. Bake for 1 hour. Bread is done when it thumps when you tap it with a finger. Let rest for 5 minutes, then remove from pan and put on rack to cool. Makes 4 loaves.

From the University of California:

Tillie Taylor's Zucchini Bread

Preheat oven to 350° F.

3 **eggs**
1 **cup peanut or safflower oil**
1 **teaspoon cinnamon**
½ **teaspoon cloves**
1 **teaspoon baking soda**
2 **cups sugar**
1 **teaspoon vanilla**
1 **teaspoon salt**
¼ **teaspoon baking powder**
2 **cups grated zucchini**
3 **cups sifted flour**
1 **cup pecans**

Beat eggs in mixing bowl until foamy. Add all other ingredients plus 2 tablespoons of water; blend thoroughly.

Spoon into two greased 9″ x 5″ loaf pans. Push batter to sides of pan, leaving a "hole" or shallow depression in the middle.

Bake for 1 hour and 20 minutes, or until a toothpick stuck down into the center of the loaf comes out clean.

From the University of Pittsburgh:

Cuban Water Bread Variation

The fastest bread recipe I know. Twelve loaves can be done in 2–2½ hours if you're lucky and kitchen is warm.

2 **packages active dry yeast**
2 **tablespoons sugar**
2 **cups lukewarm water**
6 **cups flour**
   (I use: 2 cups whole wheat flour
   4 cups unbleached white)
1 **tablespoon salt**

1. Dissolve the yeast, sugar, and salt in ½ cup warm water.

2. Add about 2 cups of flour to the rest of the warm water. (If using a mixture of flours, you can either mix them together first, or else keep track of how much of what you added.) Mix to form relatively smooth "batter."

3. Add yeast, mix in 4 more cups of flour to form a stiff dough.

4. Turn out on flat surface and knead, adding flour as necessary to keep from sticking, until smooth and elastic (5–10 minutes).

5. Let rise in warm place (we use the radiator in winter) until doubled in bulk (in greased bowl . . . grease the top of the dough, too) for 1–1½ hours.

6. Punch dough down. Divide into 2 balls. Place balls on greased cookie sheet sprinkled with cornmeal or bread crumbs or whole wheat flour. Cover and let rise for *5 minutes only.*

7. Cut fairly deep cross on top of each ball. If desired, brush with cold water and sprinkle with sesame seeds.

8. Place in *cold oven.* Set oven at 400° F. and place pan of boiling water on floor of oven.

9. Bake for 45 minutes. Loaves are done when they sound hollow when tapped with finger.

From Prescott College:

Yoga Banana Bread

Preheat oven to 350° F.

3 cups flour (whole wheat or unbleached white)
1 teaspoon baking soda
½ teaspoon salt
1½ cups brown sugar
4 bananas
½ cup yogurt
½ cup butter, cut in small pieces
2 eggs beaten

Sift together dry ingredients. Mash bananas with yogurt, add sugar, butter, and beaten eggs, and blend thoroughly. Add dry ingredients and mix well. Bake in greased pan 1 hour. Makes 1 loaf.

From the University of California at Los Angeles:

My Bread

This is the best bread recipe on the West Coast. It may be subjected to countless improvisations and innovations. I got it from a good friend, she got it from a semi-itinerant hitchhiker who called it "my bread" because it's anybody's and everybody's.

Preheat oven to 350° F.

Cook 10 minutes until dry or soft:

2 cups water
1½ cups cracked wheat

Add together with a mixture of:

3 cups water and
1 cup dry milk

Bring to boil and take from the fire.

Add:

¼ cup molasses
¾ cup honey
2 tablespoons salt
4 tablespoons oil

Cool mixture to room temperature.

Add:

3 packages dry yeast
1 cup wheat germ
1½ cups sunflower seeds
3 cups rye flour

Stir until smooth. Add 3 cups whole wheat flour. Stir it all. Add 2 to 3 cups more wheat flour. Work in with hands or spoon or both until smooth. Dough should be elastic. Fill 2–4 greased breadpans (depending on size) to about ¾" from top. Let rise to ¼" to 1" above pan. This will take 3–5 hours depending on how warm the kitchen is. Bake for 30 minutes or until loaves sound hollow.

From the University of Texas:

Popovers

Preheat oven to 450° F.

1 cup flour
1 cup milk
1 tablespoon butter, melted
¼ teaspoon salt
2 eggs

Grease muffin tins very thoroughly. Blend first 4 ingredients. Then beat in eggs one at a time. Fill muffin tins ¾ full. Bake at 450° F. for 15 minutes; turn oven down to 350° and bake for another 30 minutes. And *don't* peek! You will have deflated popovers if you do.

From Vassar College:

Molly Hall's Bread

Preheat oven to 450° F.

5½–6 cups warm water
1 cup cheapest powdered milk
1 package dry yeast
2–4 tablespoons sugar
1 tablespoon salt
5-lb. bag unbleached flour
2 tablespoons shortening (any grease will do)

Mix in gargantuan bowl with greased hands. Knead until smooth and elastic. Place in warm oven (70–80° F.) to rise to twice its bulk. Punch down after 4–6 hours. Divide into 2 balls. Divide in half. Shape and put into 4 breadpans (greased if not Teflon). Let rise for another hour or so. Bake at 450° F. for 15–20 minutes. Reduce heat to 350° F. and bake another 15–20 minutes. Take out of oven and pans. Butter crust immediately. Let cool, preferably on racks, for at least an hour if you can wait . . . hot bread is delightful, but hard as hell to slice.

A few innovative notes:
   After mixing in bowl—grease the dough with bacon grease (for flavor and to maintain moisture).
   Before baking—grease dough again while in breadpan with anything.
   Other ingredients—use imagination to alter flavor of bread. I've used packaged vanilla pudding

in ingredients and had good results. Sour cream for quasi-sour dough; more sugar or molasses for a sweeter bread.

For a richer crust, take bread out of oven after first 15 minutes, brush on a mixture of eggs, sugar, and vanilla . . . makes it sweet.

I've found this a very dependable recipe for bungling cooks like myself. Nice thing about it is that it makes four good-sized loaves—leave one out and put the other three in the freezer, as is, no wrapping necessary

From the University of New Hampshire:

Butter Dips

These go even faster than popcorn if you put out a plateful.

Preheat oven to 450° F.

1 stick butter
2¼ cups flour
4 teaspoons baking powder
¼ cup sugar
½ teaspoon salt
1 cup milk

Blend all ingredients. Roll out in rectangle on floured board. Slice with floured knife into 32 slices. Melt 1 stick butter in oblong pan and place slices in pan with edges together. Bake for 12 minutes.

From Texas Christian University:

Hot Cinnamon Puffs

Preheat oven to 350° F.

5 **tablespoons butter**
½ **cup sugar**
1 **egg**
1½ **cups flour**
2¼ **teaspoons baking powder**
¼ **teaspoon salt**
¼ **teaspoon nutmeg**
½ **cup milk**
cinnamon sugar

Cream butter, sugar, and add egg. Sift dry ingredients and add alternately with milk. Baked in greased muffin tins, small size, 8 to 10 minutes. While still warm, roll in melted butter, then in cinnamon sugar. These do not brown as they are cooked, so doneness cannot be judged by color. Makes a quick treat. Only once have I had any problems. I filled the muffin tins too full and ended up with gooey-topped puffs.

From Boston University:

Brown Bread

It's quick . . . no yeast. Preheat oven to 350° F.

Combine:

   2 eggs, well-beaten
   1 cup sugar
   ¼ cup shortening
   ⅔ cup molasses
   1 cup sour milk (or 1 cup
     regular milk + 1 tablespoon vinegar)

Sift together:

   1½ cups flour (white)
   1 teaspoon salt
   1 teaspoon soda

Add:

   1½ cups graham or whole wheat flour

Mix gently. Add:

   ½ cups nuts
   ½ cup raisins

Put in greased bread pan and bake 1 hour.

SOUP

Recipes included and the main ingredients needed

ALICE'S STOCKPOT
Leftovers, scraps, etc.

SIMPLE VEGETABLE SOUP
Carrots, zucchini (or cabbage), canned tomatoes, turnips, celery, onions, potatoes, kidney beans, pasta

PETER'S CABBAGE SOUP
Cabbage, potatoes, carrots, onions, turnip, olive oil, tomato paste

NEW ENGLAND COD CHOWDER
Chowder cod, potatoes, onion, milk

CREAM-OF-ONION SOUP
Onions, carrot, heavy cream, milk

GAZPACHO
Cucumbers, onion, carrots, radishes, pimientos, green chili salsa, dill, lemons, tomatoes, and tomato juice

NANNY'S CHICKEN SOUP
Fowl, carrots, onions, celery, parsnips, potatoes

LYNN'S VEGETABLE-BEEF SOUP
Soup bone, beef, potatoes, onions, carrots

HOT FRUIT SOUP
Apples, peaches, cherries, plums, sour cream

SPLIT-PEA SOUP
Dried split peas, bacon, onions, celery

If you're not already a soup buff, you're missing out on a good thing. Soup is cheap, filling, nutritious, delicious, and very, very easy to make. It's also good for feeding large groups of people with no fuss (and only one pot to clean). Several students on the West Coast wrote me that they use a Japanese instant soup and like it very much. If you can find it, it has interesting ingredients and is a change from bouillon cubes. Anyone who can simmer water can make homemade soup. Just take a mixture of vegetables, cut them up fairly small, simmer for 20 minutes, add salt and pepper, a pat of butter, a bouillon cube and presto . . . soup!

Traditionally, making soup began with a stock pot. This was a big pot that stood on the back of the coal stove and simmered away constantly. Whatever was available . . . cooking water from vegetables, peelings, scraps, bones, etc. . . . was dumped into it each day. Nothing was ever wasted . . . including vitamins and minerals which today we often toss into the garbage. Obviously, the flavor was never the same twice, and it wasn't meant to be eaten just as it was; but it formed a nutritious, tasty stock or base for an endless variety of fine soups. And it was almost as handy as opening a can.

From the University of Colorado:

Alice's Stockpot

Keep large jar in refrigerator for leftovers, drained juices, cooked vegetables, etc. . . . the nutritious part we usually throw away. When full, heat and serve as it is or use as a base for soup or stew. If you don't use it all up, dump it in a pan and simmer for 10 minutes once a week or it will go sour.

From Columbia University:

Simple Vegetable Soup

A good soup to study by. Fixing the vegetables is sort of restful, it smells good cooking, and it is a meal in itself without being heavy. It's cheap, too.

½ cup *each,* diced:
   carrots, turnips, zucchini (optional), canned tomatoes, celery, onions, potatoes
1 cup kidney beans, canned or cooked
1 cup elbow macaroni (or any other pasta), cooked or raw
2 quarts of water
½ teaspoon basil
1 tablespoon butter
salt and pepper to taste

Heat butter in frying pan and toss diced vegetables in it. Cook quickly, stirring constantly, for five minutes. Add to boiling water, along with beans, pasta, and basil. Bring to boil and simmer twenty minutes. Add salt and pepper.

For a richer soup, use less water or add more of everything. If you don't have zucchini, use shredded cabbage instead.

From the University of Michigan:

Peter's Cabbage Soup

1 cabbage, shredded
1 lb. potatoes, sliced
4 carrots, sliced
3 onions, chopped
1 turnip, diced
¼ cup olive oil
½ small can tomato paste
salt to taste

Boil potatoes in 2 quarts of water. When tender, mash in the cooking water. Add all other ingredients. Simmer, covered, for 1–1½ hours. You may need to add more water to keep this soup from getting too thick, but it should be substantial and hearty.

From the University of Vermont:

New England Cod Chowder

This is traditional and I try to make it often because it is cheap and filling.

2 lbs. chowder cod (very, very cheap)
5 potatoes
1 onion, sliced
2 cups milk
¼ lb. butter
salt and pepper

Just get 2 pounds of chowder cod. Put it in a bowl of cold, salted water. It sometimes has tiny water worms in it and this will make them float to the top where you can pour them off. (If the thought of that bothers you, forget the cod and use clams instead.) Peel and dice potatoes. Boil 5 minutes in 2 cups of boiling water in a large pot. Put fish in 1 cup cold water, bring to boil, and simmer 10 minutes. Strain broth. Bone cod. Add cod and broth to potatoes and potato water, with the onion. Simmer 20 minutes. Add milk, season with salt and pepper, and heat until it starts to form little bubbles (*very* soon). Serve with a pat of butter in each soup dish.

From the University of New Hampshire:

Cream-of-Onion Soup

Most any vegetable can be turned into a cream soup. We like this one but you can substitute asparagus, carrots, or any other vegetable, almost, that you want.

2 large onions
1 tablespoon carrot, grated
3 tablespoons butter
3 tablespoons flour
1 bouillon cube
2 cups hot milk
½ cup heavy cream
1 teaspoon Worcestershire sauce
salt and pepper

Boil onions 5 minutes, drain, and chop fine. Melt butter, blend in flour, and cook for 1 minute, stirring constantly. Add boiling water, bouillon cube, grated carrot, and simmer for 5 minutes. Add hot milk and cream, Worcestershire Sauce, salt and pepper to taste, and heat just to boiling point. If you want it perfectly smooth, put in blender just before adding milk and cream. Serves 6.

From Vassar:

Gazpacho

You need a blender for this one, and you don't cook it.

2 **cucumbers**
1 **large can tomato juice**
2 **carrots**
5 **radishes**
1 **Spanish onion**
2 **lemons**
1 **jar of pimientos**
1 **can green chili salsa**
   (optional—makes it hot)
2 **tablespoons fresh dill weed**
   (cheap at any natural food store)
spices you like—sweet basil,
   oregano, coriander, thyme
3 **teaspoons black pepper**
1½ **teaspoons garlic powder**
1 **ripe tomato**

Peel the cucumbers but not completely. Cut them in small pieces. Add one cucumber at a time (blenders don't like large amounts). Add some tomato juice (makes the blender work more easily) and blend until pulp. Pour into large container . . . don't use metal! Repeat with carrots, radishes, and any other vegetable you like. Do the same with ½ the onion. The rest you dice up and just put in at the end. Add the juice of two lemons and the rest of the tomato juice. Add pimientos and salsa. Mix. Add spices. Slice the tomato and add. Refrigerate. It's best after a couple of hours when things get together and better as days go by. It's refreshing, filling, and very good for you.

From Boston University:

Nanny's Chicken Soup

You've heard of "have a little chicken soup." This is the soup. Easy and tasty and you can improvise.

1 fowl (soup chicken)
½ cup carrots, diced
½ cup onions, diced
½ cup celery, chopped
½ cup parsnips, diced
½ cup potatoes, diced

Put chicken and first 3 vegetables in cold water to cover and bring to boil. Cook ½ hour on low heat. Add salt to taste. Add last two vegetables and cook ½ hour more. Add more salt, if necessary (this soup needs a goodly amount), and serve.

From the University of Colorado:

Lynn's Vegetable-Beef Soup

This recipe doesn't give amounts of everything because it isn't critical. Figure on 4–5 cups of vegetables altogether in any combination depending on what you have. Basically, so long as you have meat, potatoes, and vegetables, you are all right.

1 soup bone
1 lb. beef cut in medium-sized chunks
   (unless a very meaty soup bone)
potatoes, peeled and cut into chunks
onions, cut up, or small ones whole
carrots, sliced
also any leftover vegetables or meat
½ teaspoon sage
½ teaspoon rosemary
1 bay leaf (remove before serving)
2 quarts cold water

Put into water and bring to boil. Turn down and let simmer. Make it in the morning and simmer it all day . . . at least for 5 hours . . . it will be ready when you come home. Serve with homemade bread.

From Barnard College:

Hot Fruit Soup

Buy left-over fruit, not perfect, late Saturday afternoon. This is the fruit I used last time, but I buy what the market has, so it's not always the same.

1 cup apples, unpeeled, cored, and quartered
1 cup peaches, unpeeled, halved
1 cup cherries
1 cup plums, unpeeled, halved
1 stick cinnamon
1 clove
1 cup sour cream
2 tablespoons flour
2 tablespoons sugar

Put fruit, cinnamon, and clove in pan with 1½ quarts of cold water. Bring to boil and simmer 25 minutes. Strain the fruit out of the soup and remove pits. Mash fruit, or puree in blender. Add enough water to make 1½ quarts of soup. Add fruit pulp. Bring to boil. Mix flour with sour cream and stir into boiling soup. Add sugar. Bring to a boil again and serve. Good poured over hot, freshly cooked boiled potatoes in a big soup bowl.

From the School of the Museum of Fine Arts:

Split-Pea Soup

A jar of this in the refrigerator beats coffee as a pick-me-up at 4:00 A.M. before the big exam. It won't let you down right in the middle, either.

1 lb. dried split peas
1 lb. bacon, uncooked
4 onions, diced
2 stalks celery, diced
2½ quarts cold water
salt, pepper to taste

Throw all the ingredients into the cold water and simmer until peas disappear or get mushy . . . or whenever it is thick enough to suit you . . . usually 3 hours. Add water during cooking if necessary to keep it from getting *too* thick. Remove bacon from pot, dry on paper towels and fry until crisp. Crumble into soup and serve whenever you like. With day-old bread (cheaper than fresh) and real butter, you have a cheap meal for four or more.

EGGS

Recipes included and the main ingredients needed

SOFT-COOKED EGGS
  Eggs

HARD-COOKED EGGS
  Eggs

FRIED EGGS
  Eggs

POACHED EGGS
  Eggs

HERBED SCRAMBLED EGGS
  Eggs, milk or cream, American cheese, herbs

JAMES OMELETTE
  Eggs, onion, green pepper, tomato, milk

ONION OMELET
  Eggs, onion, sour cream

EGG FOO YONG
  Eggs, shrimp or chicken (optional), bean sprouts, green onions, bamboo shoots, water chestnuts, green peppers

EGG SALAD
  Eggs, relish, onion

HUNGARIAN PALACSINTA
  Eggs, milk, flour, butter

PATTY'S BREAD-AND-CHEESE CASSEROLE

Eggs, bread, cheese, onions, green pepper, tomatoes

EGGPLANT EGGS

Eggs, eggplant, tomatoes

CARROT PUDDING

Eggs, carrots, light cream

EGG-AND-POTATO CASSEROLE

Eggs, potatoes, onions, American cheese, parsley

LESLEY'S CHEESE SOUFFLÉ

Eggs, bread, sharp cheddar cheese

EGGS RICHARD

Bread, eggs, Swiss cheese

CHINESE EGGS

Eggs, cooked rice, pork or chicken or ham

Eggs are useful, tasty, versatile, and very easy on the budget. They are also one of your best sources of protein. For instance, if you are a vegetarian, it is hard to plan meals that provide sufficient protein . . . even with generous use of dried beans . . . but if you add eggs to your vegetable dishes, you have no problem. It is better not to buy or use cracked eggs. Eggs are used in laboratories as culture mediums because they are such a good breeding ground for germs. As long as the shell is whole, the contents are clean, but once the shell is cracked, the egg is no longer safe.

Have eggs at room temperature when you are planning to boil them and they will be less liable to crack as you lower them into the water. If you're not sure whether an egg is fresh, drop it in a glass of water. Fresh eggs sink, old eggs float. If you're not sure whether an egg in the refrigerator is hard-boiled or raw, spin it on the counter top. A raw egg will spin in place; a hard-boiled one will spin un-evenly all over the top.

A teaspoon of water added to omelet egg mix will make the omelet more tender because it retards co-agulation of the yolks. Here is how to cook basic egg dishes:

"BOILED" EGGS

The simplest way to cook an egg is to boil it. But eggs are delicate and should never be really "boiled," so we will call them "cooked" and never let the water get hotter than simmer.

Soft-Cooked Eggs: This is the kind of egg you eat with a spoon from an egg cup. All you need is a small pan of boiling water with a pinch of salt in it . . . and your eggs. Take the pan off the burner and *slowly* lower the egg into the water with a metal spoon. Set it gently on the bottom of the pan and add the rest of the eggs one at a time. Then put the pan back on the burner and cook just under boiling (simmer). Depending on how you like your eggs, cook them as follows:

2½ minutes = soft egg
  3 minutes = medium egg
  4 minutes = egg with a yolk that is mostly hard
                         but with a slightly runny center

Hard-Cooked Eggs: Proceed as for soft-cooked but simmer for 10 minutes.

To peel hard-cooked eggs easily: as soon as the egg is cooked, put it in ice-cold water for a few minutes. Then change the water and put in fresh cold water. Do not let the eggs warm up in the water. When the egg feels cool if held in the hand, it is ready to peel or to put in the refrigerator. It will peel easily if you break the shell all around the widest part of the egg with a knife or the rim of a cup. The shell will pull apart cleanly in two halves.

But if after doing this you still have trouble peeling the eggs cleanly, your eggs are too fresh. Use eggs at least three days old for hard-cooking.

FRIED EGGS

Heat aluminum skillet (if you are using stainless steel, you cannot heat it empty, so heat it with butter already in it) and then add 1 tablespoon butter —just enough to grease the bottom of the skillet so that eggs won't stick. Tilt the pan to get butter all over the bottom. Break eggs into cup or saucer and slide, one at a time, into the butter when it is hot but not burning. Turn heat down slightly and cook until white is solid and yolks are hot (if you are not sure, touch the top of the yolk lightly with your finger. This is called "sunny side up." If you prefer, you can use more butter and spoon it over the yolk while the egg is cooking. This will turn the yolk opaque. (You can also cover the pan for a minute to get the same result.) If you want the egg for a fried-egg sandwich, turn it over with a spatula and brown the other side, breaking the yolk in the process. (Otherwise you will have egg on your chin with your first bite.) Salt and pepper to taste *after* the egg is cooked.

POACHED EGGS

Making a good poached egg always gives me a feeling of accomplishment. Especially if you do it the French way, which is to drop the whole egg (broken out of its shell into a cup) into a small pan of boiling, salted water. If the egg is really fresh, the white will wrap itself around the yolk and make a reasonably compact mass. Cook it for 3 minutes in gently boiling water and remove with a slotted spoon. An easier way is to buy an egg poacher (they come for one egg and for several). In which case, you break the eggs into the buttered metal cups which sit over boiling water. These cups keep the eggs nicely shaped so that they look handsome on a properly golden-brown piece of toast. Poached eggs are very handy. They can be served in a well on top of corned-beef hash or hot cooked spinach . . . or over a piece of broccoli and ham, etc. They will make a breakfast, lunch, or dinner . . . depending on how substantial the other things you serve are . . . and they are quick.

But the quickest, easiest way to cook eggs is to scramble them.

From Barnard College:

Herbed Scrambled Eggs

2 eggs
2 tablespoons milk or cream
½ teaspoon chopped chives or dill or tarragon
1 tablespoon American cheese
1 tablespoon butter

Beat everything together, except butter, lightly with a fork. Heat frying pan, add butter. When foam of butter starts to subside, pour in egg mixture and cook on lowered medium heat, stirring gently with your fork to "scramble." Eggs are done when they look creamy or just firm . . . do not cook them dry. The whole cooking time shouldn't take more than 3–4 minutes.

From the Curtis Institute of Music:

James Omelette

6 eggs
½ cup onion, chopped
½ cup green pepper, chopped
1 tomato, diced
½ cup milk
¼ teaspoon paprika
1 tablespoon butter
salt and pepper to taste

Beat eggs; add onions, peppers, and tomato. Pour in milk. Flavor with paprika. Pour into hot, buttered skillet and cook for 10 minutes over medium heat. Put under broiler for 3–5 minutes to brown. Replace on top of stove burner. When solidified, remove from heat. Salt and pepper to taste. Serves 2–3 average.

From Yale University:

Onion Omelet

3 eggs
1 tablespoon water
½ onion, sliced *thin*
2 tablespoons sour cream
1 tablespoon butter
salt and pepper

Break eggs in bowl and add water. Slice onions and separate into rings. Beat eggs and water lightly. Pour into small, hot, buttered skillet. Lift up edges as eggs cook and tilt pan so uncooked egg runs over the sides onto bottom of pan. When eggs are almost set, lay onion all over the top. Cook for a minute more. Just before taking out of pan, spoon sour cream over ½ of the eggs. Fold over with spatula and slide onto plate. Season.

The eggs and onions are hot and the sour cream is cold. Great!

From Union College (Schenectady, N.Y.):

Egg Foo Yong

Very filling and good . . . serve with hot rice.

6 eggs
½ cup shrimp or chicken (optional)
½ cup bean sprouts
1 cup green onions, thinly sliced
½ cup bamboo shoots, thinly sliced
½ cup water chestnuts, sliced thicker
½ cup green peppers, thinly sliced
1 teaspoon salt or 2 teaspoons soy sauce
2 tablespoons peanut oil
¼ teaspoon pepper

Beat eggs thoroughly and add other ingredients, except oil. Mix well and divide into 4 portions. Drop 1 portion into skillet with hot peanut oil. A small skillet is best, since omelet should be small and thick rather than spread out. Butter is all right if you don't have peanut oil. Brown on both sides, turning with spatula. Cook until firm. Keep cooked ones hot and cook one at a time.

Gravy (not necessary but good):
2 teaspoons soy sauce
1 teaspoon sugar
1 teaspoon vinegar
½ cup cold water
1 teaspoon cornstarch

We use cornstarch because it keeps the sauce translucent in real Chinese style but you can use any thickener you like. Put all the ingredients in small saucepan and cook over low heat until thick. Pour over each serving of Egg Foo Yong.

From Curtis Institute of Music:

Egg Salad

6 eggs
1 tablespoon mayonnaise
¼ teaspoon mustard
½ teaspoon relish
½ teaspoon onion, chopped
salt and pepper to taste

Hard-cook 6 eggs. Separate yolks and white and chop. Mix the yolks with mayonnaise and mustard. Add relish, onions, and chopped egg whites. Use more mayonnaise if necessary to bind. Salt and pepper.

Note: The eggs can be either hot or cold when you use them.

From the University of Connecticut:

Hungarian Palacsinta

These are what some people call crêpes.

3 eggs
2 cups milk
1½ cups flour
1 tablespoon confectioners sugar
½ teaspoon salt
1 tablespoon melted butter
6 teaspoons melted butter

Beat eggs until frothy. Add sugar, 1 tablespoon melted butter, salt, milk, and flour, beating in as you add. Batter must be about the consistency of melted ice cream.

Brush pan thickly with melted butter for each "crêpe." When butter is hot, spoon in 2–3 tablespoons of batter and quickly rotate pan so that the batter spreads evenly and thinly over the bottom. A 6"–8" pan is best.

Brown quickly, then turn to brown other side. Stack cooked "crêpes" in a flat dish with waxed paper in between. They can be made in advance and stored in the refrigerator until needed.

To use, fill with cottage cheese, jam, fruit, or ice cream; roll up and sprinkle with sugar and cinnamon. Lobster or crab newburg also makes a good filling (hot).

These are suitable for any meal—breakfast, lunch, or dinner—depending on what you put in them.

From the University of California at Los Angeles:

Patty's Bread-and-Cheese Casserole

Preheat over to 350° F.

6 **slices bread**
2 **cups grated cheese (cheddar or whatever you like)**
2 **onions, thinly sliced**
1 **green pepper, chopped**
3 **tomatoes, sliced**
salt, pepper
½ **cup butter**
1¼ **cups milk**
2 **eggs**

Use sliced wholewheat or left-over bread of any kind . . . stale or otherwise. Toast and cut into smaller pieces. Put layer of bread, layer of cheese, layer of vegetables. Salt and pepper. Dot with butter or sprinkle with any salad oil, except olive oil, if you don't have butter. Repeat until everything is used up. Heat milk and beat in eggs. Pour over whole thing. Bake for about 40 minutes or until milk has been absorbed and cheese is melted and bubbly. Very good . . . very easy.

Finely chopped green onions are really good in this.

From Mills College:

Eggplant Eggs

A really inexpensive dish that tastes expensive. Filling enough for dinner if you serve two to a person.

8 slices eggplant, about ½ʺ thick
**   (use small eggplant)**
3 tablespoons butter
3 tomatoes, sliced thickly (use left-over ends
**   and very small slices in salad some time)**
8 eggs
½ cup bread crumbs
salt, pepper

Bread eggplant and sauté in butter until brown. Set aside but keep hot. Grill tomato slices under broiler for 2 minutes on each side but be sure they do not get soft. (If no broiler, dip in bread crumbs and fry quickly in butter for 1 minute on each side.) Keep hot. Fry eggs, keeping each one separate from the others. Cover each eggplant slice with a tomato slice (use slices big enough to cover the eggplant) and top with fried egg. Season. This takes only one pan and very little time.

From the Peabody Conservatory of Music:

Carrot Pudding

Preheat oven to 325° F.

3 eggs
3 cups carrots, grated
2 cups light cream
¼ cup flour
1 teaspoon salt
¼ teaspoon pepper
½ teaspoon mace
4 tablespoons butter, melted

Beat eggs until frothy. Stir in carrots. Mix together flour, salt, pepper and mace. Stir into egg mixture. Add melted butter and cream and stir for 3 minutes. Pour into buttered casserole and set in pan of boiling water. (Add more water if necessary during cooking to keep water about 1 inch up sides of casserole.) Bake approximately 1½–2 hours. Pudding is done when a knife inserted in the center comes out clean. If there is custard sticking to it, it isn't done yet.

From Boston College:

Egg-and-Potato Casserole

Preheat oven to 400° F.

mashed potatoes, seasoned
hard-cooked eggs, sliced
onions, sliced and in rings
American cheese, grated
butter
paprika, salt, pepper
minced parsley

Quantity depends on size of baking dish and how many you want to make this for. In a buttered pie plate, layer ingredients in this order: potatoes, eggs, onions, cheese. End up with a layer of potatoes and dot with butter and paprika, salt and pepper to taste.

Bake in oven ½ hour. Sprinkle parsley over just before serving. Serve in pie plate . . . it looks interesting . . . then take out each portion.

From Hobart College:

Lesley's Cheese Soufflé

Not so difficult as most soufflés because it doesn't collapse easily. Prepare the day before.

12 slices white bread
½ cup butter, softened
1 lb. sharp cheddar cheese, grated
¼ cup melted butter
2 cups milk
1 teaspoon salt
1 teaspoon dry mustard
¼ teaspoon pepper
4 eggs

Remove crusts from bread and butter well. Cube. Put bread and grated cheese alternately in greased baking dish. Beat remaining ingredients with egg-beater (not electric) and pour on bread and cheese. Place in refrigerator for at least 24 hours. Remove 1 hour before baking. If in a glass dish, bake one hour at 300° F. . . . metal dish one hour at 325° F.

From Boston College:

Eggs Richard

Preheat oven to 400° F.

6 slices bread, fresh or stale
6 slices Swiss cheese
6 eggs
butter
nutmeg
salt, pepper

Cut crusts off bread. Fry one side only in butter until brown. Put slices of fried bread flat in greased baking dish or cookie sheet. Lay a slice of cheese on each slice of bread. Break an egg onto cheese. Some of the white will run over but the yolk should stay on. You can press down a little in the middle of the cheese, if necessary. Sprinkle with salt, pepper and nutmeg, and bake until eggs are done.

From Union College (Schenectady, N. Y.):

Chinese Eggs

1 **cup minced pork or chicken or ham**
3 **cups cooked rice**
1 **tablespoon butter**
6 **eggs**
2 **tablespoons soy sauce**

Heat meat and rice in skillet in butter. Add soy sauce. Add beaten eggs and stir all together. Keep stirring and cook until eggs are done.

GROUND BEEF

Recipes included and the main ingredients needed

COCIDO
Ground beef, potatoes, green beans, chick peas, sausage

FAIRLY CHEAP CHILI
Ground beef, pinto beans, tomato sauce, enchilada sauce, onions

HAMBURGERS HAWAIIAN
Ground beef, onions, soy sauce, ginger

MEAT LOAF
Ground beef, onions, eggs, ketchup

STUFFED PEPPERS
Ground beef, onion, mushrooms, rice, tomato sauce, green peppers, cheddar cheese

PEPPER BALLIES
Homemade or canned chili, onions, cheddar cheese, corn chips

MIKE'S CHILI
Ground beef, kidney beans, onions, green peppers, tomato paste, canned tomatoes

CHINESE PEPPER GROUND STEAK
Ground beef, tomatoes, green peppers, ginger, cornstarch

SHARI'S GRINDERS
Ground beef, egg, onions, Parmesan cheese, bread crumbs, Italian sausage, tomato sauce, green peppers

SWEET-SOUR MEATBALLS
Ground beef, pineapple tidbits, brown sugar, cornstarch, water chestnuts, green pepper

ENCHILADA CASSEROLE
Ground beef, flour, enchilada sauce, olives, tortillas, onions, grated cheese

TASTY BURGERS
Ground beef, brown sugar, onions, chili sauce, celery

BEEF AND PINTO BEANS
Ground beef, pinto beans, tomato sauce, onion

SPOONBURGERS
Ground beef, onions, green pepper, rice

BEEF STROGANOFF
Ground beef, garlic, onions, paprika, mushrooms, sour cream

CHEESEBURGER CASSEROLE
Ground beef, onion, American cheese, broad noodles, canned tomatoes

ZUCCHINI DINNER IN A DISH
Ground beef, zucchini, canned tomatoes, onion

HAMBURGER NOODLE CASSEROLE
Ground beef, onions, noodles, cottage cheese, sour cream

RED BEANS, RICE, AND BEEF
Ground beef, onions, kidney beans, stewed tomatoes, sherry

DANISH BARBECUE HAMBURGERS
Ground beef, beer, Worcestershire sauce, vinegar

TACOS
Ground beef, taco shells, onion, tomato sauce, cheddar cheese

Hamburger (or ground beef) is comparatively cheap, so you eat it often. But it is so versatile there is no reason it should ever be boring. It has another big advantage over other inexpensive cuts of meat . . . it can be cooked quickly without the long hours of braising that are needed to make most cheap cuts tender. Another virtue of hamburger is the way it can be stretched . . . less meat and more vegetables or pasta can be a boon when cash runs low or there are more than expected to dinner.

Cook it as if you care and you will dine well no matter how thriftily.

From New York University:

Cocido

This is what Spanish peasants often eat. Serve with hard-crust bread, wine, and a green salad.

6 potatoes, peeled and cut in quarters
1 lb. green beans, cut in 1″ pieces
1 can chick peas, drained
1 lb. chopped round steak or chopped stew meat
½ lb. spicy sausage, sliced
1 garlic clove, minced
1 onion, chopped
1 teaspoon mint
(or several minced fresh sprigs)
1 bouillon cube
salt & pepper to taste

Add potatoes and green beans to 2 quarts boiling salted water and simmer 25 minutes. Add chick peas last 5 minutes. While vegetables are cooking, brown chopped meat with garlic and onion. Remove, drain pan, and fry sliced sausages 8 minutes. Drain off fat, add chopped meat and sausage to vegetables (when vegetables are tender). Simmer 10 minutes. Serve in two courses. Soup is the liquid drained off the meat and vegetables plus one bouillon cube and seasoning to taste. You can add a cupful of cooked rice or any pasta if you like. Main course is meat and vegetables. You can serve each ingredient piled separately on the plate or all together. If you wish to serve them separately (and that means cooking them separately), you have to use a lot more pots. To make more or less than this recipe, keep proportions roughly equal except for less sausage (proportionately).

From the University of New Hampshire:

Fairly Cheap Chili

Lasts a long time and it's hot because we like it that way. Great stuff! It's fairly cheap because you can use less meat and more beans without it making all that much difference.

1 lb. pinto beans
2 lbs. ground chuck
1 8-oz. can tomato sauce
2 10-oz. cans enchilada sauce (hot)
lots of chili powder (4 or more teaspoons)
lots of chopped onions (5–6)

Boil up beans in 8 cups water until tender (takes time!). You will probably have to add more water before they are done. Sauté chuck and onions, drain off all fat before adding to drained cooked beans. Add sauce and chili powder and stir all together. Simmer for as long as you like.

From the University of Louisville:

Hamburgers Hawaiian

1 lb. ground beef
1 medium onion, minced
1 clove garlic, minced
½ cup soy sauce
¼ teaspoon ginger

Mix beef and onion and shape into 8 patties. Put in shallow baking dish. Combine remaining ingredients and pour over patties. Let stand 30 minutes, turning once. Drain and broil or pan-fry. Serve with sliced pineapple.

From Vassar College:

Meat Loaf

Lots of people don't like meat loaf but we do because it's tasty, easy to make, and good cold in sandwiches.

Preheat oven to 350° F.

1 cup water with 1 bouillon cube dissolved
3 onions, chopped
2 lbs. ground beef
2 eggs, beaten
¼ to ½ cup ketchup
1½ cups soft bread crumbs
¾ cup warm water
salt and pepper

Brown onions in a little fat. Add water and bouillon cube and simmer 5 minutes. Mix together in a bowl with all other ingredients. Salt and pepper to taste. Mix thoroughly. Shape into loaf and place in loaf pan or shallow baking dish. Bake 1 hour.

From the School of the Museum of Fine Arts:

Stuffed Peppers

Preheat oven to 325° F.

1 lb. ground beef
1 onion, chopped
1 lb. mushrooms, sliced
1 cup cooked rice
2 cups tomato sauce
3 green peppers, cut in half and seeded
cheddar cheese, grated

Mix first 5 ingredients together and stuff into peppers. Set upright in pan and bake 30–45 minutes.
Last 5 minutes, take out and dot with cheddar cheese. Stick back in oven until cheese melts.

From the University of Denver:

Pepper Ballies

This is a favorite at the Antelope Valley Fair in Lancaster, California, every September.

1 can chili (or your own)
½ lb. cheddar cheese, grated
1 onion, chopped
corn chips

Heat chili until very hot. Grate cheese. Chop onion.

In individual bowls, put down a layer of chips. Spoon chili over these. Cover with a layer of cheese (it'll melt). Add onion to taste.

We serve this with red wine and a loaf of bread with the rest of the cheese melted on it.

From the School of the Museum of Fine Arts:

Mike's Chili

If you buy chili in cans, it's almost all beans. This is better and cheaper, and you can make extra to keep in the refrigerator and heat up when someone is hungry.

2 lbs. ground beef
2–3 medium onions, chopped
2 cans kidney beans, drained
1 green pepper, chopped (optional)
1 teaspoon tomato paste
2 1-lb. cans whole tomatoes
2 teaspoons chili powder
salt, pepper, to taste

Brown meat and onions in skillet. Drain off fat. Add kidney beans, green pepper, tomato paste, tomatoes, and seasonings. Simmer covered about ½ hour —longer if time is available.

From Rice University:

Chinese Pepper Ground Steak

You can make this with sliced steak, but this way we can afford to have it oftener and it tastes just as good.

1½ lbs. ground beef
¼ cup butter
1 garlic clove, minced
3 tomatoes, chopped
4 green peppers, seeded and cut into strips
¼ cup soy sauce
¼ teaspoon pepper
½ teaspoon sugar
1½ teaspoons ginger
1¼ cups hot water with bouillon cube
2 tablespoons cornstarch

Shape meat into small patties and brown with garlic in butter. Add tomatoes and green peppers. Add seasonings and all liquids except ½ cup beef bouillon mixture. Cover and cook for 20 minutes. Mix cornstarch with remaining beef stock and stir into meat mixture. Simmer for a few minutes until thickened, stirring constantly. Serve with hot rice.

From the University of Bridgeport:

Shari's Grinders

Meatballs:
½ lb. ground beef
1 egg
1 onion, minced
2 teaspoons garlic salt
3 tablespoons parsley flakes
½ cup Parmesan cheese, grated
1 cup bread crumbs
salt and pepper to taste

Mix all ingredients together and shape into balls.

½ lb. Italian sausage (sweet and hot, mixed), sliced
3 cans tomato sauce
4 large green peppers, cut in narrow strips
2 medium onions, cut in narrow strips
2–3 tablespoons salad oil

Brown meatballs and sausages in oil. Remove from pan. Sauté onions and pepper in same oil until soft. Add meat mixture and tomato sauce and simmer ½ hour, covered, stirring once or twice.

Spoon into grinders or pita bread.

From the New England Conservatory of Music:

Sweet-Sour Meatballs

These should be served with hot, cooked rice, so make some along with the rest of the recipe.

1 lb. ground beef
1 cup bread crumbs
1 bouillon cube
1 cup pineapple tidbits
¼ cup brown sugar
3 tablespoons cornstarch
¼ cup cider vinegar
1 teaspoon soy sauce
1 5-oz. can water chestnuts, drained
  and thinly sliced
1 green pepper, cut in strips

Mix meat and bread crumbs with salt and pepper as you like it, and form into medium-sized meatballs. Sauté until well-browned on all sides. Add ½ cup hot water and bouillon cube. Cover and simmer ½ hour.

Drain pineapple, reserving syrup. In medium saucepan, combine brown sugar and cornstarch. Blend in pineapple syrup, ½ cup water, vinegar, and soy sauce. Cook and stir over low heat till mixture thickens. Gradually stir in meatballs, with their pan gravy, water chestnuts, green pepper, and pineapple. Heat to boiling. Serve over rice. Garnish with tomatoes. Serves 4.

From the University of New Hampshire:

Enchilada Casserole

This one is great!

2 lbs. ground beef
3 tablespoons oil
3 tablespoons chili powder
1½ teaspoons salt
oregano
½ cup flour (or less)
2 small cans enchilada sauce
½ cup water
2 cups sliced olives
2 dozen tortillas (approx.)
grated cheese
chopped onions

Brown meat in oil. Add chili powder, salt, oregano, and flour. Go easy on the flour . . . see how thick you like it (it thickens as it cooks). Add liquids and simmer 10 minutes. Add olives, reserving a few. Simmer 2–3 minutes more. In large greased casserole, place layer of meat mixture with *quartered* tortillas. Add ½ of remaining meat mixture and generous amounts of cheese and onion. Then another layer of tortillas and remaining sauce. Finish with cheese and onions and rest of sauce. Bake for 30 minutes. This freezes well.

From the University of Louisville:

Tasty Burgers

1 lb. ground beef
1 tablespoon brown sugar
2 tablespoons fat
2 tablespoons onion, diced
2 tablespoons celery, diced
¾ cup chili sauce
1 teaspoon prepared mustard
1 tablespoon vinegar
½ teaspoon salt

Brown meat in fat. Add rest of ingredients and simmer till done. Spoon onto warm hamburger buns, and serve.

From the University of Pittsburgh:

Beef and Pinto Beans

1½ cups pinto beans
1 onion, chopped
2 cups hot tomato sauce with chili to your taste
1 lb. ground beef

Cook pinto beans until soft. Mush them up (we use our hands—it's kind of fun in an old "mud pie" consciousness kind of way), add some of the chopped onion and sauce and refry for a while . . . about 10 minutes. Brown hamburger with the rest of the onions and, when brown, add hot sauce. Serve beans and hamburger with fresh tomatoes and shredded lettuce. You can serve with taco or burrito shells (fried in oil) and piled all together with a side dish of guacamole and it's a good meal (especially with cold beer). If you like it really hot, add a few hot peppers in the cooking.

From Columbia University:

Spoonburgers

1 lb. ground beef
2 onions, sliced
1 green pepper, chopped
½ cup chicken broth
¼ cup cooked rice
¼ teaspoon dry mustard
2 tablespoons ketchup
salt and pepper to taste

Brown beef and onion in small amount of fat in frying pan. Add peppers and cook 3 more minutes. Mix broth, rice, mustard, ketchup.Pour over mixture of meat and onions and peppers. Simmer 10 minutes and serve over rice or toast or hotdog roll.

From Vassar College:

Beef Stroganoff

1½ lbs. ground beef
½   cup onions, sliced
½   cup butter
1   clove garlic on toothpick
2   tablespoons flour
1   lb. fresh mushrooms, sliced
1   cup chicken broth
1   cup sour cream
2   teaspoons salt
¼   teaspoon pepper
dash paprika

Brown beef and onions in butter with garlic. Sprinkle with flour and toss in frying pan. Add seasoning and rest of ingredients. Heat thoroughly, stirring frequently. Serve over hot rice. Serves 6–8.

From the School of the Museum of Fine Arts:

Cheeseburger Casserole

1   lb. ground beef
1   onion, grated
2   teaspoons butter
1½   cups broad noodles, cooked
1   can tomatoes without juice (optional)
1   cup American cheese, diced

Crumble hamburger and onion in hot butter in skillet, and brown. Add drained hot noodles and toss. Add tomatoes. Stir in cheese. Cook about 10 minutes or until cheese bubbles.

Variation: Also good with left-over ham and diced pineapple . . . omit cheese and tomato and use ½ cup pineapple juice.

From William Smith College:

Zucchini Dinner in a Dish

Only one pot to wash for a really good dinner.

1 cup onion, chopped
2 lbs. chopped beef
3 medium-sized zucchini, sliced
2 No. 1 cans whole tomatoes
2 tablespoons parmesan cheese, grated
1 clove garlic, minced

Brown onions and meat together. Drain fat. Add remaining ingredients. Cook at medium-low heat for 45 minutes on top of stove. Salt and pepper to taste. Serve sprinkled with grated parmesan cheese. Serves 6–8.

From the University of Pittsburgh:

Red Beans, Rice, and Beef

This recipe can be made with one hot plate and one electric (or nonelectric) frypan in 30 minutes (with practice).

¾ lb. ground beef (type depends on how much you over-spent last week. If beef is lean, you may need to use some fat . . . we keep fat from bacon, soup, etc., in a can on the stove)

1–2 white onions, chopped

½ teaspoon thyme ⎫ or whatever seasonings
½ teaspoon marjoram ⎭ you prefer

chili powder (start with a teaspoon and work up to your taste)

1 large can kidney beans (1 to 1½ lbs., depending on how far meat has to be stretched)

1 large can stewed tomatoes (can also use tomato puree, which will make a thicker sauce)

sherry to taste

Fry beef, onions, and seasoning until meat is brown and onions are clear. Add kidney beans and tomatoes. I mix this with my hands . . . but you can use a bowl and a spoon. Simmer for however long you have . . . at least 20 minutes. Serve over hot rice. Serves 4.

N.B. Most stores, from time to time, sell day-old mushrooms at *very* low prices. These can be sautéed with onions and meat (omit chili powder) for an entirely different dish. And the mushrooms are good (if you like mushrooms) in almost anything . . . except they're really a little far "gone" for a salad.

From the School of the Museum of Fine Arts:

Danish Barbecue Hamburgers

½ **cup beer**
2 **lbs. ground beef, shaped into patties**
½ **cup ketchup**
2 **tablespoons Worcestershire sauce**
2 **tablespoons vinegar**
½ **teaspoon salt**
¼ **teaspoon pepper**

Pour out beer and let stand at least 15 minutes before using. Meanwhile, brown hamburger in small amount of fat in frying pan. Mix together beer and all other ingredients. Pour over hamburger and let simmer for 10 minutes or until hamburger is done.

From Vassar College:

Hamburger Noodle Casserole

Preheat oven to 300° F.

8 oz. noodles, cooked
1 lb. ground beef
1 medium onion, chopped
1 lb. cottage cheese
1 pint sour cream
grated parmesan cheese
salt and pepper to taste

Cook noodles and drain. Keep hot. Grease casserole baking dish and set aside. Brown hamburger in skillet. Add onion and seasoning, and cook until onion is tender. Drain fat from meat mixture and combine in casserole with noodles, cottage cheese and sour cream. Cover with parmesan cheese (sprinkled over top as thickly as you like) and bake for 30 minutes. Serves 4.

From the University of California at Los Angeles:

Tacos

This is taco shells (tortillas fried in oil and folded in half) with meat filling.

6 taco shells
1 lb. ground beef
1 large onion, diced
1 cup hot sauce (tomato sauce heated with chili powder or canned chili sauce)
½ cup cheddar cheese, grated
salt and pepper

Prepare taco shells by frying tortillas in oil and folding in half. Brown meat and onions in small amount of fat. Spoon into folded tacos, cover with sauce, sprinkle with grated cheese. Serve with shredded lettuce and tomato salad and a bottle of tabasco for those who like it hotter than you made it.

BEEF

Recipes included and the main ingredients needed

SWEDISH CASSEROLE
Stew beef, cabbage, turnips, molasses

SHISH KABOB WITHOUT THE KABOB
Stew beef, green peppers, tomatoes, onions, barbecue sauce

SCANDINAVIAN BEEF LIVER
Beef liver, prunes, apples, milk

BRAZILIAN BEEF CASSEROLE
Stew beef, potatoes, celery, green pepper, coffee, wine

SUSANNAH'S BEEF STEW
Stew beef, carrots, celery, potatoes, tomato sauce or tomatoes

Meat is your best source of complete protein—unfortunately, it is also the most expensive. However, since the cheapest cuts are just as good . . . sometimes even better . . . for you than the most expensive, patience and cooking skill really pay off. Most inexpensive cuts of meat require longer, slower cooking, but their flavor is as good as the costliest cuts and they lend themselves to a lot more variety. The longer cooking time isn't really an inconvenience, because it doesn't mean hanging around and watching it. Once it is in the oven or on the stove, simmering away, you can forget about it until it is ready.

From Texas Christian University:

Swedish Casserole

Preheat oven to 350° F.

2 **lbs. stew beef or some inexpensive cut, in chunks**
1 **medium cabbage, chopped coarsely**
2 **turnips, sliced**
2 **tablespoons molasses**
¼ **teaspoon marjoram**
2 **tablespoons caraway seeds**
2 **teaspoons salt**
2 **cups hot water**

Turn everything into a casserole or skillet and either bake in a 350° F. oven or simmer slowly on top of stove for 1½ hours. Serve with mashed potatoes.

From Union College (Schenectady, N. Y.):

Shish Kabob
Without the Kabob

This is fast, easy, delicious. We like to serve it with curried rice. It feeds a mob but you can cut it down as much as you like.

6 green peppers
6 tomatoes
6 medium small onions
5 lbs. stewing beef, cut in chunks
4 jars barbecue sauce with mushrooms
   (or make your own)

Cut peppers, tomatoes, onions into eighths. Put in large bowl or bowls and add meat and sauce. Toss until everything is completely coated with sauce. Marinate for 3 hours (or more, if convenient . . . even overnight is o.k. in the refrigerator). Line cake pan with foil, place meat and vegetables in rows in pan . . . as if on a skewer but without the skewer. Pour on marinade liquid from bowls. Broil, turning once, approximately 15 minutes. Test for doneness by cutting into one piece of meat.

Serves approximately 20 people . . . or fewer if you cut down on all the ingredients.

From Boston College:

Scandinavian Beef Liver

This is great for people who think they don't like liver.

Preheat oven to 350° F.

6 slices beef liver
2 cups cooked prunes, pitted and chopped
8 apples, peeled, cored, sliced
milk
salt, pepper to taste

Butter casserole. Wash liver, remove outside skin and membranes. Slices must be uniform and large enough to roll. Don't settle for bits and pieces or ends. Lay liver slices flat on wax paper and almost cover with prunes and apples. Roll slices up with prunes and apples (like a jelly roll) and skewer with toothpicks. Lay in casserole and pour in milk until it just covers the meat. Bake until milk is absorbed and completely disappears. Very good served with yams.

From Boston University:

Brazilian Beef Casserole

If you don't want to simmer this on top of the stove, it can just as easily be done in the oven. Cover and don't let cook above simmer.

2 lbs. stew beef in chunks
4 potatoes, quartered
2 stalks celery, sliced
1 green pepper, chopped
1 cup strong coffee
1 clove
1 teaspoon cinnamon
¾ cup sweet or dry wine (to your taste)
¼ cup flour

Sear meat in a little butter or fat. Combine all other ingredients, except flour, and simmer approximately 45 minutes to 1½ hours, or until meat is tender. Sprinkle flour gradually into stew, stirring constantly. Or mix small amount of sauce with flour in separate bowl, then add to pot. Cook, stirring, until slightly thickened.

From Vassar College:

Susannah's Beef Stew

2½ lbs. beef-stew chunks
7 carrots, sliced
4 stalks celery, sliced
6 potatoes, quartered
2 beef-bouillon cubes, dissolved
   in 2 cups boiling water
1 large can tomato sauce or tomatoes
   (tomatoes will make it thinner)
1 bay leaf
salt, pepper to taste

Place everything in casserole, cover and bake for 2½–3 hours. If you use tomato sauce, you may need to add a little more liquid.

Since this tastes even better the second or third day, we sometimes make it ahead. It is easily heated up and makes a great leftover. Serves 5–6.

VEAL

Recipes included and the main ingredients needed

BREADED VEAL PATTIES
 Veal patties, bread crumbs, eggs

SUNDAY-BEST VEAL BREAST
 Breast of veal, onion, celery, heavy cream, noodles

VEAL PATTIES IN SOUR CREAM
 Veal patties, sour cream, onions

OSSO BUCO
 Veal knuckles, celeriac, onion, carrots, garlic, wine, tomato paste, lemon, parsley

STUFFED BREAST OF VEAL
 Breast of veal, bread, onions, raisins, sesame seeds

VEAL AND MUSHROOMS
 Shoulder or breast of veal, mushrooms, onions, canned tomatoes, sour cream

VEAL PARMESAN (Almost)
 Veal steaks, tomato sauce, mozzarella cheese

VEAL TERIYAKI
 Stewing veal, sesame oil, soy sauce, sherry, garlic, ginger

SAUTÉED VEAL AND TOMATOES
 Stewing veal, onions, garlic, canned tomatoes, lemon juice, black olives

Veal is a nice change from other meats and is very different in flavor and recipe possibilities. It is not used nearly so much in this country as in Europe, and gourmets will tell you that the finest veal, known as "white" veal, is next to impossible to buy here any more. However, you will find veal that works perfectly well in almost any market. Just look at it carefully to make sure it doesn't look dried-out or sort of gray. It should be pink—the lighter the better—a gray look or gray areas (even a little one) means it's been sitting around too long.

Veal patties, always sold frozen, are a combination of veal and beef ground up together and shaped into very thin patties. They cook up very, very quickly but they contain a lot of fat, so allow at least 2 to a serving.

From Vassar College:

Breaded Veal Patties

Take patties out of wrapping and separate. Thaw for a few minutes. While thawing, combine bread crumbs with oregano, basil, and parsley. Add salt and pepper to taste.

Beat 2 eggs in a bowl. Dip patties in eggs, then coat quickly with bread-crumb mixture and fry immediately in butter or olive oil.

The number of patties depends on how many you are feeding and what else you are serving. Two eggs will bread a lot of patties.

From the University of Colorado:

Sunday-Best Veal Breast

On Sundays people are liable to drop in unexpectedly and hang around till it's time to eat. If you've
got the makings, this is quick and can be stretched
to feed a mob.

**2 lbs. breast of veal, cut into 4″ squares
   (more if you expect company)
4 cups hot water
1 onion, minced
1 stalk celery, minced
2 teaspoons salt
pepper
3 teaspoons Worcestershire sauce
½ teaspoon dry mustard
¼ lb. uncooked noodles
   (we like the broad ones) (more for company)
¼ cup flour
3 cups butter
½ cup heavy cream**

The day before: Put veal, water, onion, celery, and
salt in a large pan and cook until meat is tender
. . . about 1½–2 hours. Cool until you can handle
the meat. Then slip out the bones and cut in about
2″ pieces. Put back in the broth and refrigerate until
you are ready to use it (it will keep a couple of days
easily).

To make this takes about ½ hour: You need 4 cups of broth, so measure what you have and if it comes out less, add water to bring it up to 4 cups. Put in large pan and add salt, pepper, Worcestershire sauce, and mustard. Bring to a boil and add noodles. Cook until tender (15–20 minutes, depending on what kind of noodles you are using). *Do not drain.*

Meanwhile, dredge meat in flour and brown well in any hot fat or oil (not olive) in large frying pan. When noodles are tender, add cream to them and toss. Heat to boiling. Arrange browned meat on a large platter and pour noodles and sauce over it. Do not mix. Serve.

This serves 6–8 but you can easily double it without any more work and serve 16.

From Columbia University:

Veal Patties in Sour Cream

Fry veal patties until cooked (about 7 minutes, turning once). Save fat. Remove and keep hot. Fry chopped onions in fat until light brown. Add sour cream and enough water to make a thin sauce. Add cooked patties and whatever herbs and seasoning you like. Cover and simmer for 5–10 minutes until sauce is desired thickness. Add a little soy sauce, if you like.

From Union College (Schenectady, N.Y.):

Osso Buco

6 veal knuckles, good-sized with lots of meat
2 tablespoons butter
2 tablespoons olive oil
2 tablespoons tomato paste
½ cup celeriac, grated
1 onion, chopped
3 carrots, grated
2 garlic cloves, minced
½ teaspoon rosemary
½ teaspoon oregano
1 cup dry wine (red or white)
1 lemon, juice and grated rind
3 tablespoons parsley, minced
salt and pepper

Brown knuckles in butter and oil on all sides. Then arrange them with the bone vertical (so the marrow won't fall out). Mix tomato paste with ½ cup hot water and add together with all the other ingredients *except* wine, parsley, and lemon juice and rind. Cover and simmer for 1½ to 2 hours, until veal is tender, adding more hot water, if necessary. Add rest of wine, lemon juice and rind, salt and pepper the last 10 minutes. Serve with rice sprinkled with parsley. Serves 6.

From the Peabody Conservatory of Music:

Stuffed Breast of Veal

This feeds as many people as there are ribs. Since the breasts of veal seem to vary in size, we can't give exact quantities. Buy a breast of veal that has a pocket. Before you stuff it, make the pocket larger with a sharp knife so it will hold more stuffing.

Preheat oven to 325° F.

Wash breast of veal by putting under water faucet and then pat with paper towels. Mix salt, pepper, garlic salt, and oregano and rub it inside and out veal breast.

To make stuffing: crumble up a loaf of bread (more or less depending on size of pocket), some browned chopped onion, raisins, sesame seeds, thyme, sage, and salt and pepper. Pour melted butter over it and mix thoroughly with your hands. Stuff into pocket, but don't make the stuffing layer too thick. Cover (with foil is all right) and cook for 1½ hours. Uncover and bake another ½ hour or until brown (if very dry, use a little butter to help it brown).

From William Smith College:

Veal and Mushrooms

2½ lbs. shoulder or breast of veal,
   cut in pieces
2 tablespoons butter
1 teaspoon salt
1 tablespoon paprika
¼ teaspoon cayenne
8 mushrooms, sliced
4 onions, chopped
2 tablespoons rye flour
1 small can tomatoes
1 cup sour cream
½ cup hot water

Brown meat in butter. Add seasonings. Add mushrooms, onions and cook 5 minutes. Sprinkle on flour and stir. Cook 5 minutes, stirring occasionally. Add all other ingredients and cover and simmer for 1½–2 hours, adding more water, if necessary.

From the University of Denver:

Veal Parmesan (Almost)

Preheat oven to 350° F.

6 veal steaks, breaded
3 tablespoons olive oil
1 8 oz. can tomato sauce
½ lb. mozzarella cheese, sliced
1 teaspoon oregano
Parmesan cheese, grated
salt and pepper

Fry steaks until well browned in olive oil. Place in baking dish. Salt and pepper to taste. Pour tomato sauce over steaks. Top with mozzarella. Sprinkle with oregano and Parmesan. Bake for about 25 minutes or until cheese is bubbling and browned a bit. Serves 6.

From the University of Miami:

Veal Teriyaki

Marinade:
½ **cup sesame oil**
¼ **cup soy sauce**
½ **cup medium sherry**
2 **garlic cloves, minced**
2 **tablespoons ginger**
½ **teaspoon cayenne**
salt, if necessary

3 **lbs. stewing veal**
⅔ **cup flour**
4 **tablespoons butter**
2 **tablespoons sesame oil (optional)**

Cut veal in more or less uniform cubes (stewing veal comes in all shapes and thicknesses). Combine marinade ingredients and pour over veal. Marinate at least 3 hours (even overnight is OK).

Pat veal dry and dredge with flour. Brown in hot butter in skillet. When all sides are brown, add marinade to skillet. Simmer gently, covered, for about 1 hour or until veal is tender. If more liquid is needed, add a little hot water as necessary. If you accidentally add too much, thicken with cornstarch.

A few minutes before taking off the fire, stir in sesame oil.

Good over any kind of pasta, especially broad noodles.

From Tulane University:

Sautéed Veal and Tomatoes

The meat is inexpensive but you'd never know it from the taste.

3 lbs. stewing veal
1 cup flour
6 tablespoons olive oil
4 tablespoons butter
2 onions, chopped
3 garlic cloves, minced
1 large can Italian tomatoes
1 large can (tomato can) hot water
½ cup red wine (optional)
¼ cup lemon juice
2 teaspoons basil
1 teaspoon oregano
2 cups pitted black olives, sliced
salt and pepper to taste

Cut veal in more or less uniform pieces. Dredge with flour and brown in skillet in oil and butter. When brown on all sides, add onions and garlic to veal and sauté 10 minutes, stirring once.

Add tomatoes and ½ can of hot water. As liquid heats up, stir and scrape bottom of pan to get off all stuck-on brown bits.

Add rest of ingredients. If less than ½" of liquid, add rest of hot water. Keep ½" liquid all through cooking. Simmer, covered, until meat is tender, about 1½–2 hours. Pour sauce from pan over veal when serving.

LAMB

Recipes included and the main ingredients needed

EASY LAMB STEW
Lamb, carrots, potatoes, onions, garlic, canned tomatoes

LAMB CURRY WITH YOGURT
Lamb, onions, zucchini, carrots, yogurt

IRISH LAMB STEW
Lamb, onions, carrots, turnips, potatoes

ENGLISH LAMB STEW
Lamb, potatoes, celery, parsnips, zucchini, tomato sauce

ENGLISH HOT POT
Breast of lamb, lamb kidneys (optional), potatoes, mushrooms (optional), onions

BARBECUED BREAST OF LAMB
Breast of lamb, onion, barbecue sauce

LIBYAN COUSCOUS
Lamb, canned Italian tomatoes, chick peas, onions, tomatoes, pine nuts, Italian tomato paste, garlic, couscous

MOUSSAKA
Lamb, eggplant, onion, tomato sauce, mozzarella cheese (optional)

LUBI AND RICE
Lamb, onion, green beans, canned tomatoes, rice

138

SWEET-AND-SOUR STUFFED CABBAGE
Lamb, cabbage, rice, onions, tomatoes, tomato
paste, ginger snaps

Lamb has a special flavor all its own. It appeals to
tastes as different as English and Arabic; lends itself
equally well to bland dishes or to highly spiced ones.
Australian lamb is different from American lamb in
that it is more strongly flavored. . . but delicious. . .
and is a different shape.
Australian leg of lamb is longer and narrower, with
the result that sometimes it will not fit into your roasting pan. If it looks too long, have the butcher cut off
the end and then use it for soup (with barley). Since
Australian lamb is much less expensive than American lamb, it is a good buy when you can find it. It usually comes frozen, so plan ahead so it has time to thaw
thoroughly. Although all lamb has gotten much more
expensive lately, there are still relatively inexpensive
cuts, and these are easy to cook. Breast of lamb is
about the cheapest cut and it's fine if you remember
to remove the fat after cooking. The easiest way is to
cook it the day before and pick the congealed fat off
before reheating. Stewing lamb is good for many
dishes, but it has bones, so you need more than you
might think to make a meal of it. Sometimes you can
get a "special" at the market on leg of lamb. If you do,
bone it (very, very easy with a boning knife) and cut it
up into chunks. It comes out much cheaper than stew
meat and is all meat.
　　Lamb chunks are also good for shish kabob and all
sorts of braised dishes. If you don't need a whole leg
for a roast, ask the butcher (even in a supermarket) to
cut off three or four chops and that will give you two

meals . . . broiled chops one night, roast lamb a few nights later. Or ask him to cut lamb steaks (which come from the center of the roast instead of the end), which are very very expensive to buy and should be used for a really special meal. Then bone the rest yourself for lamb chunks. Always use the bones for soup. Chopped lamb is as useful as hamburger. It makes patties, shish kabob, stuffed cabbage, and many Middle-Eastern dishes. Keep it in mind as a change from chopped beef.

From Union College (Schenectady, N.Y.):

Easy Lamb Stew

This has so much broth, it's practically soup . . . a very solid, hearty, filling soup . . . and should be served in big bowls. Use more vegetables and less meat if you overspent the week before.

Preheat oven to 350° F. (or you can even make it on a hot plate).

3 lbs. boned leg of lamb (or 5 lbs. stew meat)
10 carrots, cut in chunks
8 potatoes, cut in chunks
10 small onions (I use canned ones)
2 cloves garlic, minced
2 teaspoons salt (taste when done,
   may need more)
1 teaspoon pepper
2 small cans tomatoes (optional)

Put everything in a large casserole (or a couple of medium-sized ones). Fill with water until everything is about an inch under water. Put foil in oven underneath casserole in case it boils over. Put casserole in oven and forget about it for 1½ hours. Look at it once to make sure it isn't boiling too hard, in which case turn it down a little. Serves 8. Reheats in half an hour the next day.

From Goddard College:

Lamb Curry with Yogurt

This recipe can be made with all vegetables (and no meat). Time would be only an hour to cook the whole thing.

2 lbs. lamb, cut up
1 cup onions, chopped
4 tablespoons curry powder (hot)
2 bouillon cubes
2 fresh zucchini, cut up
4 carrots, cut up
1 carton yogurt
salt, pepper, garlic salt to taste

Brown meat and onions. Throw into a large pot. Add curry, 3 cups of water, bouillon cubes. Simmer for one hour or until meat is tender. Add more water and another bouillon cube if necessary. Add vegetables. Cook 10 minutes. Add yogurt. Simmer 1 hour more. Taste and add more curry if you wish. Serves 8 with rice.

From the University of New Hampshire:

Irish Lamb Stew

Eating is an event, a time to be together, to enjoy each other, the creation that has been made, a time to enjoy, also a time to be quiet and digest and enjoy to the fullest. This is a dish for four friends.

2 lbs. stewing lamb
¼ cup flour
3 tablespoons fat
2 teaspoons celery seeds
3 tablespoons parsley, minced
8 small onions
8 carrots
8 potatoes
4 turnips
salt, pepper to taste

Dredge lamb in seasoned flour. Save left-over flour. Sauté lamb in fat until very brown all over. Add water and all other ingredients, except vegetables. Sprinkle on flour and blend in. Add all vegetables and cover. Simmer 1 hour or until meat is tender. Serves 4. Or maybe 6. After that, increase the ingredients and serve as many as you like.

From Vassar College:

English Lamb Stew

Preheat oven to 225°F.

1 **large can tomato sauce**
½ **can water**
½ **teaspoon salt**
½ **teaspoon pepper**
½ **teaspoon dry mustard**
1½–2 **lbs. lamb (leg or boned shoulder**
  is good), in chunks
2 **cups potatoes, in chunks**
1 **cup celery, in chunks**
4 **parsnips, in chunks**
4 **zucchini, in chunks**
2 **teaspoons minute tapioca**

Mix tomato sauce and water with seasonings. Put everything else in roaster or casserole and pour tomato sauce mixture over it. Stir to mix.

Bake for 5 hours (I put it together in the morning and we eat it when we come home . . . not necessarily all together). Serves 6.

From George Washington University:

English Hot Pot

Very filling and no trouble.

2 lamb kidneys (optional)
6 potatoes, sliced
3 onions, sliced
2 cups mushrooms, sliced (optional)
1½ lbs. breast of lamb, trimmed of fat and cut into rib-
　lets
1½ cups bouillon or stock
2 tablespoons butter
salt, pepper

Remove any skin from kidneys, cut away fat. Soak in cold salted water 20 minutes. Slice ¼″ thick. Grease casserole large enough to hold all the ingredients comfortably. Put in layer of potatoes, then lamb and kidneys, then onions. Continue in this order but end up with a layer of potatoes. Dot surface with butter. Pour in bouillon. Bake for 2 hours. Cover for first 1½ hours. Then uncover to brown top.

　Keep an eye on it toward the end to make sure it doesn't get too dry. If necessary, add more liquid (pour down side, not over potatoes). Serves 6–8.

From the Peabody Conservatory of Music:

Barbecued Breast of Lamb

Almost as tasty as spareribs . . . only much cheaper.

2–3 lbs. lamb breast
1 medium onion, sliced
2 tablespoons vinegar
1 tablespoon sugar
1 teaspoon rosemary
½ teaspoon dry mustard
salt, pepper

Simmer lamb, onion, vinegar, sugar, rosemary, and mustard in large pot with water to cover for 1 hour. Drain. Cut into riblets and dry with paper towels. You can do this the day before you want to eat it. Then dinner takes 15 minutes to make.

Make barbecue sauce (or use bottled). Cover shallow pan with foil and lay meat on it. Brush with sauce and put under broiler. Broil 5 minutes on each side, brushing with sauce to keep moist. Serve with hot extra sauce in a dish. We serve it with rice. Serves 6 with vegetables and a salad.

From Columbia University:

Libyan Couscous

I throw in *lots* of fat—this really adds flavor, is usually cut out by Westerners. This takes time to make but it is really worth every minute of it.

10 large onions, chopped
4–5 lbs. leg or shoulder of lamb, cut in
    large cubes (I like Australian lamb for this)
1–2 cups olive oil
2 large cans Italian tomatoes
5, 10, or 15 garlic cloves, chopped
1 can Italian tomato paste
2 teaspoons turmeric
2 teaspoons curry
1 teaspoon fresh ground pepper
5–15 crushed cardamon pods (optional)
10 large potatoes, quartered
handful of pine nuts
2 or 3 cans chick peas
5–10 zucchini or yellow squash, cut in
    large pieces
2 1-lb. boxes couscous

This takes at least 8 hours, preferably overnight, for the first steps:

1. Brown onions and lamb in lots of olive oil. Add garlic and brown. At the end of browning, add tomato paste, pine nuts, turmeric, curry, and pepper. If you can get it (Middle-Eastern food stores carry it.) add 1 teaspoon of harissa for mild, 2–3 for hot (and genuine)

couscous . . . this stuff is really potent. I didn't include it in the regular list of ingredients because it
might be hard to get.

2. Put browned mess into large pot. Add tomatoes,
crushed cardamon pods, and enough water to cover
everything. Bring to a boil, then turn down low and
simmer, covered, either overnight or from about 2:00
P.M. to 6 or 7:00 P.M. (Harissa gets hotter the longer
it cooks, so if you have used that, better start tasting
about 6:00 P.M.)

3. About 3 hours before you plan to finish cooking,
add chick peas; 1½ hours, add potatoes; 1 hour, add
squash. (A kitchen-timer is good if you are studying in
between.)

4. Follow directions on package for couscous. Or
do it my way: takes 3 hours. Wash for 3 minutes in
cold water, let stand in bowl for 1 hour. Then put it in
strainer or cheesecloth, steam for 1 hour. (If you have
room in the pot you are cooking the rest of the stuff
in, put couscous in sieve or strainer and steam over
that . . . covered). Take out, wash in cold water,
drain. Mix in olive oil with your fingers so you can
feel it covering all grains, break up any lumps. Steam
for another hour.

5. When couscous is steamed, put in the serving
bowls. Mix in 1–3 cups of liquid and fat from stew
so it all looks orange red. Do it fast. Then pile the
stew on top. Then everyone gathers round and eats it
with fingers or large spoons—it's meant for gorging
on.

From the University of California (Santa Barbara):

Moussaka

Preheat oven to 375° F.

1 lb. lamb, chopped or minced
1 eggplant, in ½ "thick slices
1 onion, minced
½ cup tomato sauce
½ cup water
1 cup parsley, minced
¼ lb. butter (1 stick)
salt and pepper

Brown lamb in butter in frying pan (not all the butter, just as much as you need). Add onion and cook until translucent. Add tomato sauce, water, and parsley. Cook 5 minutes. Remove and keep hot in sauce.

Brown eggplant, adding more butter. Put half of eggplant slices in baking dish. Top with meat mixture. Top with another layer of eggplant. Bake for 45 minutes.

Note: It isn't really at all proper but I like to add a cup of chopped mozzarella cheese over the top. It gets all bubbly and a little brown (add it 10 minutes before the dish is done). This is sort of combining Greek and Italian cooking!

From the New England Conservatory of Music:

Lubi and Rice

An easy Arabic dish.

2 cups rice
1½ tablespoons butter
1 lb. lamb, ground or chopped fine
1½ teaspoons pepper
1 teaspoon salt
1 onion, chopped
1 lb. green beans, cut up
1 small can tomatoes

Wash rice 3 times in lukewarm water. Drain and cover with boiling water. Let stand one hour, then drain.

Put butter (1 tablespoon for each cup of rice) in heavy pan. Melt till hot but do not burn. Add rice and sauté for 15 to 20 minutes, until brown and crisp (slightly). Add some salt. Cover with warm water. Cover pan tightly, bring to boil, turn down heat and cook until dry.

While rice is cooking, brown meat, seasoning, onion in butter. Add beans, cook 15 minutes more. Add tomatoes plus 1 can of water (water should cover, add more if necessary). Cook, covered, over low heat for ½ hour. Serve meat mixture over rice.

From New York University:

Sweet-and-Sour Stuffed Cabbage

1 large cabbage
2 lbs. chopped lamb
1 cup cooked rice
1 large onion, chopped
salt and pepper to taste
2 cans tomato paste
2 small cans tomatoes
8 tablespoons vinegar
10 ginger snaps, crumbled
½ cup vinegar
⅓ cup brown sugar
4 bay leaves
2 cups water

Cut hard center core out of cabbage. Cook in boiling water 10 minutes . . . or until you can peel off outer leaves without breaking and they are soft enough to roll without cracking. (Take a few off at a time with a pair of tongs; put aside to cool. Then take the next few off, etc.)

While cabbage is softening, mix meat, rice, onion, and salt and pepper together gently. Do not compress the meat if you can help it. Add about 2 teaspoons tomato paste and mix in. Put as much of this mixture into each cabbage leaf as it will comfortably hold in the stem end. Roll over once, tuck in sides, roll closed and fasten with two round wooden toothpicks used as skewers. Put in bottom of large pan and then on top of one another. When all the stuffing is used up (some of the leaves get quite small near the end), cover them with the rest of the ingredients . . . ginger snaps first and then everything else poured over. Cover and cook slowly for 4 hours. Tastes even better the second day. Freezes well. Serves 10.

CHICKEN AND OTHER POULTRY

Recipes included and the main ingredients needed

EASY CHICKEN CURRY
Broiler or fryer, curry powder

CHARLES'S CHICKEN VERONIQUE
Broilers, broth, white wine, white grapes

ELAINE'S CHICKEN CACCIATORE
Broiler or fryer, spaghetti sauce, stuffed Spanish olives, tomato sauce, wine

PAM'S CHICKEN AND MUSHROOMS
Broiler, eggs, milk, bread crumbs, mozzarella cheese, mushrooms

CHICKEN AND OLIVES
Fryer, canned tomatoes, olives, wine

CHARLIE'S CHICKEN CORDON BLEU
Chicken breasts, sliced ham, cheddar cheese, Swiss cheese, bread crumbs

CHICKEN LIVERS AND TOMATOES
Chicken livers, onions, tomatoes, soy sauce

CAROL'S BARBECUED CHICKEN
Broiler or fryer, peach preserves

MARINATED CHICKEN
Chicken, olive oil, spices

NORALYN'S CHICKEN
Broiler, soy sauce, peanut oil, spices

ELLEN'S SESAME CHICKEN
Broiler or fryer, sesame seeds, white wine

MABLE DESMOND'S CHICKEN
Broiler or fryer, onions

NEW ORLEANS CHICKEN
Fryer, canned tomatoes, onion, celery, green pepper

PINEAPPLE CHICKEN
Chicken breasts, cooked rice, pineapple chunks, raisins

ROAST TURKEY
Turkey, bread, onions, butter

GARLIC CHICKEN
Broiler, garlic

ERIC'S CHICKEN AND TOMATOES
Broiler or fryer, stewed tomatoes, onions

Chicken is so inexpensive you can afford to eat it often. It lends itself to a wide variety of dishes— from bland to hot—and is the most versatile of all leftovers. All poultry is very perishable and should be refrigerated promptly even when cooked. If you have a large amount of chicken in a pot of broth or soup, take out all the chicken and other solids, put in a tightly covered container and refrigerate. Put the pan of broth in cold water (in the sink is o.k.) and keep the water cold by changing when necessary. Do this for about 15 minutes and then refrigerate. Never just let it stand on a counter or stove until it cools off.

If you are planning to roast a stuffed turkey, do not stuff it until just before you put it in the oven.

You can make the stuffing the day before, but don't put it inside the turkey. *Never, never* stuff it the day before.

Chicken comes in many different forms and you need to know the differences if you are to buy wisely.

Broilers: Small, tender chickens, usually under three pounds. Good for broiling, all right for roasting whole. Chicken parts are usually cut-up broilers or fryers and are a very expensive way to buy chicken. However, if you want just boned chicken breasts for a particular recipe, bone them yourself and save a lot of money. It is very easy. Ask your butcher to show you, get a book out of the library, or just buy a good boning knife and try to cut the meat off the bones by running the knife right along the bone, separating the bone from the meat as you do so. The boning knife pays for itself the first time you use it.

Fryers: Just like broilers only somewhat bigger. They stand up better for frying because they don't dry out so quickly. Fine for broiling, too. Also for all casserole dishes.

Roasting chickens and capons: Good for roast chicken or casseroles.

Hen, fowl, stewing chickens: Best for soup, boiled chicken, etc. If you try to make soup out of a broiler, it won't have much flavor. (If this happens, cheat a little and add a chicken bouillon cube.) A really nice 5–6 pound fowl cooked for 3 or 4 hours is your best bet for soup or stock.

Caution: All chickens (except parts) come with giblets, which are heart, liver, gizzard, and neck. Hunt for them. In a roast chicken, they will be found packed inside somewhere; sometimes sneakily in the neck cavity, sometimes in the other end. If you absent-mindedly roast the chicken without removing the giblets and the paper they are wrapped in, the results may be inedible. Take them out and save them for making giblet gravy or giblet stew or to enrich chicken stock.

To roast poultry in foil, turn the oven 25° F. higher than your recipe calls for. Open up the foil during the last third of your cooking time and baste occasionally to brown. For safety's sake, though, put the foil-wrapped package in a pan . . . otherwise you may spill the drippings when you lift the foil out of the oven at the end of cooking.

From Barnard College:

Easy Chicken Curry

This is a good recipe for other kinds of meat, too.
   Preheat oven to 400° F.

1 broiler or fryer, cut in pieces
½ cup butter, melted
1 teaspoon curry powder
salt and pepper to taste

Bake chicken, seasoned with salt and pepper, in oven or broiler/oven for 35 minutes, turning 2 or 3 times to brown evenly. Mix butter with curry and pour over chicken just before serving. Serve on bed of hot cooked rice.

From the University of Vermont:

Charles's Chicken Veronique

Very good with tossed salad and rice (or noodles).

2 broilers, cut up
¼ cup salad oil
¼ cup flour
1 teaspoon salt
1 teaspoon rosemary
¼ teaspoon black pepper
¼ teaspoon thyme
1 garlic clove, minced
1 bay leaf
1½ cups chicken broth
¼ cup milk or cream
¼ cup flour
½ cup white wine
3 cups white grapes (can be canned)

Brown chicken in hot oil in skillet. Remove pieces as they brown. Drain left-over oil and add chicken broth to skillet. Stir in salt, rosemary, pepper, thyme, garlic, bay leaf.

Mix 1 tablespoon of cornstarch with milk or cream and stir it into broth until broth thickens. Add chicken and simmer, covered, for 40 minutes. Add more broth if sauce gets too thick, but remember to allow for the wine. When ready to serve, add wine and grapes and just heat through.

Serves 6–8.

From Boston College:

Elaine's Chicken Cacciatore

My special creation that takes almost no time to prepare, is inexpensive, tastes delicious!
Preheat oven to 350° F.

1 fryer or broiler, cut in pieces
¼ cup olive oil
1 clove garlic, minced
1 medium jar spaghetti sauce
1 large can tomato sauce
1 small jar stuffed Spanish olives
½ teaspoon oregano
½ teaspoon basil
1 teaspoon onion salt
10 oz. inexpensive Chianti wine

Salt and pepper chicken and sauté in olive oil and garlic until golden-brown. When well browned, remove and keep hot in baking dish.

While chicken is sautéing, put spaghetti sauce, tomato sauce, olives (and olive juice), spices, and wine in saucepan. Heat to simmering and pour over chicken. Bake for 25 minutes.

Serves 4, 5, or more depending on the budget.
. . . I often use this as a side dish with spaghetti. If you can afford it, serve as a main dish with the spaghetti on the side. The sauce can be stretched to accommodate as much spaghetti as you need for unexpected company by adding more Chianti and a small can of tomato paste.

From the University of Vermont:

Pam's Chicken and Mushrooms

A really good recipe for chicken.
  Preheat oven to 475° F.

  De-bone a broiler (cheaper than buying it cut up and it only takes a minute!).
  Pound pieces flat. Make a batter of 2 eggs and 1 cup of milk, beaten together. Dip chicken in egg mixture, then in bread crumbs. Fry in hot butter until golden brown—about 15 minutes.
  Put browned chicken in greased baking dish. Top with mozzarella cheese and sautéed mushrooms (or canned button mushrooms, sliced and heated).
  Top with buttered bread crumbs. Place in oven and bake until cheese is melted and bread crumbs are golden brown.

From the University of Denver:

Chicken and Olives

Great if you like olives as much as we do.

1 fryer, cut up
¼ cup olive oil
1 can tomatoes or 1½ cups chopped fresh
  tomatoes

1 garlic clove, minced
1 can pitted black olives or 1 bottle
   stuffed olives
2–3 tablespoons sherry, Chablis, or sauterne

Brown fryer in olive oil. Add tomatoes, garlic, olives, and wine. Cover and simmer for ½ hour.

From the University of Vermont:

Charlie's Chicken Cordon Bleu

The more cheese the better. Just double ingredients to serve more. For a party, serve lots of rice.
   Preheat oven to 350° F.

4 chicken breasts, boned
½ lb. sliced ham, coarsely chopped
¼ lb. cheddar cheese, shredded
½ lb. Swiss cheese, shredded
1 cup bread crumbs
1 teaspoon tarragon
salt and pepper to taste
3 tablespoons butter

Pound breasts flat. On each breast place a layer of ham, then cheddar and Swiss cheese. Roll and secure with toothpicks. Place in butter-greased baking dish and dot with butter. Sprinkle with bread crumbs mixed with tarragon. Bake for 40 minutes.

From Columbia University:

Chicken Livers and Tomatoes

1 lb. chicken livers
2 small onions, sliced thin
3 tablespoons butter
3 tomatoes, cut into small pieces
1 tablespoon vinegar
1 tablespoon soy sauce
salt and pepper to taste
½ teaspoon garlic or cumin or cloves or ginger
    or coriander or curry powder

Separate each liver into 2 pieces. (This is natural, as you will see when you look at the livers.) Slice onions thin and fry in butter until yellow. Add livers and sauté, stirring frequently. Add tomatoes. Add water if necesary to keep from burning. Add vinegar, soy sauce. Season as desired. Add enough water to keep some liquid in the pan, and simmer, covered for 8 minutes.

If you want to serve this over rice or spaghetti, make more sauce by adding more water and some tomato paste and you will have as much sauce as you need. (You may have to add more seasoning; in this event, just taste as you go along.) Substitute mushrooms for onions if your budget will stand it.

From Boston University:

Carol's Barbecued Chicken

This is great! Preheat oven to 350° F.

1 broiler or fryer, cut up
¼ cup melted butter (you may need more)
½ teaspoon barbecue sauce (bottled is fine)
½ teaspoon garlic salt
And the Secret Ingredient:
** 1 teaspoon peach preserves**

Place chicken in shallow pan. Coat with sauce of all other ingredients mixed well together. Bake 45 minutes to 1 hour. If you like, turn on broiler and broil the last 10 minutes of cooking time to make browner. Be sure to spoon liquid in pan over chicken every 15 minutes or so.

From New York University:

Marinated Chicken

Make a marinade of olive oil, salt, pepper, oregano. Put in pieces of chicken (a broiler cut up), and refrigerate for 1–2 hours, turning occasionally.

Put chicken in 350° F. oven for 30 minutes and baste with marinade as it is cooking. Pour pan juices over chicken when you serve it.

From the University of Denver:

Noralyn's Chicken

This is an easy recipe for a party—just double or triple the ingredients. It's quick to make once the chicken is marinated. And even the rice can be made ahead of time and reheated.

Cut up a broiler. Marinate 2–3 hours, or even overnight, in soy sauce, peanut oil, minced fresh ginger, minced garlic cloves, dry mustard, lemon juice, and a little salt.

Drain chicken and broil as usual, brushing with the marinade a couple of times while cooking. Five minutes before chicken is ready, sprinkle with chopped peanuts. The marinade can be heated and served in a separate dish along with the juice in the broiling pan. Serve with a big bowl of rice. Serves 4–6.

From the University of Pittsburgh:

Ellen's Sesame Chicken

Preheat oven to 400° F.

1 **broiler or fryer, cut up**
1 **cup buttered bread crumbs**
1 **cup white wine**
½ **teaspoon thyme**
1 **cup sesame seeds, toasted**
salt and pepper to taste

Arrange broiler in shallow baking dish. Pour wine over chicken. Mix bread crumbs, sesame seeds, thyme, salt, and pepper. Sprinkle over top of chicken. Bake 1 hour.

Note: Most sesame seeds are not toasted when you buy them. We toast a batch in the oven and keep them handy for cooking.

From Boston University:

Mable Desmond's Chicken

Excellent soul cuisine! Preheat oven to 350° F.

1 broiler or fryer, cut up
2 large onions, chopped
1 cup water
seasoned salt, enough to sprinkle over chicken

Place cut-up chicken pieces in a flat pan. Sprinkle with seasoned salt and onions. Pour water into one corner of pan (not over chicken or all the seasoning will be washed off). Cover with foil unless pan has its own cover. Simmer on top of stove ½ hour (2 burners if large pan). Then put in oven for 1 hour, adding water if necessary (keep checking). Uncover last 15 minutes to brown.

From the University of Texas:

New Orleans Chicken

1 fryer, cut up
1 cup flour
3 tablespoons butter
1 large onion, chopped
2 stalks celery, chopped
1 green pepper, chopped
1 can tomatoes
1 cup boiling water
1 teaspoon sugar
1 tablespoon Worcestershire sauce
Salt and pepper to taste

Flour chicken and sauté until golden-brown on all sides. Remove and keep hot.

Put in onion, celery, and green pepper. Cook, stirring constantly, 5 minutes. Add tomatoes, boiling water, sugar, Worcestershire sauce, and seasonings. Simmer 5 minutes. Put chicken in sauce, cover, and let simmer 1¼ hours. Thicken gravy with cornstarch, if desired, and serve with rice.

From Vassar College:

Pineapple Chicken

A budget dish that makes a good one-dish company meal.

Preheat oven to 350° F.

2 cups cooked rice
pineapple chunks—reserve 1 cup juice
raisins
3–4 chicken breasts, cooked, in chunks
butter
brown sugar
1 tablespoon soy sauce

Grease a deep casserole dish. Then layer with rice, pineapple chunks, raisins, chicken. Dot with butter and sprinkle with brown sugar. Repeat layering until ingredients are used up. Mix pineapple juice with soy sauce and pour over layered ingredients. Bake till heated through—about ½ hour.

What's good about this dish . . . can use left-over rice, chicken. Be as skimpy with the chicken as you want to be. Can toss in nuts.

From the University of New Hampshire:

Roast Turkey

I never knew it was so easy to make roast turkey until I tried! It makes a great company dinner and turns into all sorts of quick, easy dishes (curried, creamed, hash, etc.) if there is any left over.

Preheat oven to 350° F.

1 turkey, ready for roasting
salt and pepper

Stuffing:
fresh or slightly stale bread
onions, sliced
butter, melted
sage, thyme, salt, pepper

I can't give exact amounts for stuffing because it depends on the size of the turkey. A 10-lb. turkey needs a whole loaf of bread, 3 onions, 1½ sticks of butter, 1 teaspoon each sage and thyme. Actually the amounts are not critical . . . the stuffing always tastes good and smells heavenly anyhow. Some small turkeys seem to hold more stuffing than others. Put stuffing in the neck cavity too. If you have more than will fit into the turkey, put it in buttered custard cups, cover with foil, and put it in the oven the last hour the turkey is roasting.

To make stuffing: crumble bread into small pieces (I like this better than crumbs). Sauté onions in a little of the butter until golden brown. When onions are done, swirl *all* the butter into the pan to pick up the onion flavor. Mix the stuffing ingredients together with your hands in a big bowl.

To roast turkey: rinse turkey under faucet, body cavities, too. Dry with paper towels, and salt, inside and out. Stuff.

Put turkey in preheated oven and roast for 25 minutes a pound, basting occasionally with pan juices. (Put a little water in the pan to begin with so you have juices sooner and it doesn't all stick to the bottom of the pan. I line the pan with foil . . . it seems to save more gravy.)

You can easily tell when a turkey is done. Put a fork into the part where the leg attaches to the body. If the juice that runs out is pink, it isn't done. If it is yellow or golden, it is done. But don't do this until the leg moves easily when you jiggle it. If you do it more than one or twice, you will drain all the juice out of your turkey and make it dry.

From the University of Denver:

Garlic Chicken

Chicken needs variations because we eat it so often. The memory of this one stays with you.

Preheat oven to 350° F.

Put a cut-up broiler in a shallow dish. Add a lot of butter (dotted all over) and minced garlic (lots—like two or more cloves). Cover with aluminum foil and bake for 1 hour. Uncover the last 15 minutes of cooking so it will brown.

From the University of Pittsburgh:

Eric's Chicken and Tomatoes

Preheat oven to 400° F.

a broiler or fryer, cut up
2 cans stewed tomatoes
2 onions, minced
2 cups mushrooms, sliced (optional)
½ tablespoon marjoram *or* sage
3 tablespoons butter
1 cup sherry (optional)
salt and pepper

Put chicken in casserole and dot with all the butter. Sprinkle with herbs and salt and pepper. Bake 30 minutes, then add remaining ingredients and bake another 30 minutes.

The sherry and mushrooms are optional . . . it depends on whether or not we can afford them.

FISH

Recipes included and the main ingredients needed

FISH FILLETS IN WHITE WINE
Fish fillets, lemon, white wine

FISH SCALLOP
Fish fillets, onion, Swiss cheese, sour cream, sherry, currants, walnuts

SHRIMP 'N' RICE
Shrimp, onion, safflower oil, garlic, sauterne

BAKED STUFFED HADDOCK
Haddock fillets, sesame seeds, shrimp, butter, white wine

TUNA-VEGETABLE MIX
Canned tunafish, brown rice, peas, canned corn

BAKED FLOUNDER IN SOUR CREAM
Fish fillets, sour cream, mushrooms, mayonnaise

PATTY'S JAMBALAYA
Onion, hot sausage, tomato sauce, shrimp, garlic, green pepper, parsley

TUNAFISH CASSEROLE
Canned tunafish, peas, onions, green peppers, lemon juice, white sauce, mushrooms, spaghetti, sherry

BAKED HERBED FISH
Fish fillets, spinach, almonds

SALMON AND MUSHROOM CASSEROLE
Canned salmon, brown rice, white sauce, cheddar cheese, raisins, broccoli, mushrooms

Fish is popular to eat but not to cook . . . according to many students. They find it is often impractical for the conditions under which they cook (in dorms, for instance), and they can't always find a good fish store or fish department where they market. They think, also, that fish isn't so flexible as meat; if plans change and it can't be cooked that evening as intended, they feel uneasy about keeping it for another night. Canned fish doesn't present the same problems, as I could see from the number of you who sent in practically the same recipes in this category.

From Columbia University:

Fish Fillets in White Wine

Preheat over to 350° F. Rub any fillet or fish steak (e.g. cod) with fresh lemon. Place in shallow glass baking dish. Sprinkle on salt, pepper, paprika, parsley, lemon juice. Add white wine (up to ⅓ cup, depending on amount of fish). Dot fish with butter. Bake 10–15 minutes, until fish is flaky. Serve with enough sauce to moisten.

From the University of Delaware:

Fish Scallop

Use any fish fillets. Preheat oven to 375° F.

2 lbs. fish fillets
1 onion, chopped
1½ tablespoons flour
2 cups sour cream
½ cup grated Swiss cheese
2 tablespoons butter
2 tablespoons sherry
2 tablespoons *each* currants and walnuts
½ teaspoon cinnamon
½ teaspoon allspice
1 teaspoon salt
½ teaspoon pepper
1 cup buttered bread crumbs
(bread crumbs mixed with melted butter)

Dust fish with flour and brown lightly in butter on both sides. Place in buttered casserole in layers with sauce spooned on to each layer.

Sauce: Sauté onions until translucent. Mix flour with sour cream and add along with all other ingredients, except bread crumbs, to onions. Mix well. When fish and sauce are all in casserole, cover with bread crumbs and bake 45 minutes. Serves 6.

From the University of Denver:

Shrimp 'n' Rice

Here's my favorite . . . it takes only 20 minutes. The same recipe works for sole or haddock or whatever fish you have.

½ cup chopped onion
1 tablespoon safflower oil
1 garlic clove, minced
1 bay leaf, crushed
1 teaspoon minced parsley
1½ lbs. shrimp (the frozen little ones
   do quite well)
1 cup sauterne wine
salt and pepper
1 teaspoon cornstarch

Sauté onion in oil until the onion starts to color. Add garlic, bay leaf, parsley, and shrimp. Sauté 3 minutes. Add sauterne and salt and pepper. Cover and simmer gently for 20 minutes. Thicken sauce with cornstarch which has been mixed into a paste with a little water. Simmer until sauce thickens. Serve over rice. Serves 6.

From Boston College:

Baked Stuffed Haddock

Preheat oven to 350° F.

1½ lbs. fillet of haddock slices
shrimps (one for each haddock slice)
2 tablespoons toasted sesame seeds
1 cup butter, melted
½ teaspoon turmeric
½ cup white wine
dash salt, pepper

On each slice of fish place 1 shrimp, a tiny pat of butter, and some sesame seeds. Roll up and skewer with toothpick. Lay rolled-up fish in buttered casserole. Combine melted butter, turmeric, wine, and salt and pepper. If there are any sesame seeds left, add them too. Sprinkle over fish. Cover with bread crumbs that have been mixed with melted butter. Surface should be *completely* covered with bread crumbs. Bake uncovered in oven about 30 minutes or until crumbs are quite brown. Allow 2 slices to a person.

From the University of Northern Colorado:

Tuna-Vegetable Mix

This is quick but good. Any number can eat.

brown rice
peas
corn
tunafish (canned)
onion salt
salt and pepper

Cook rice, peas, and corn separately. Heat tunafish in a little butter with onion salt. Mix vegetables together, salt and pepper to taste. Serve on plates, dump tunafish on top.

From Vassar College:

Baked Flounder in Sour Cream

A fish dish for when you tire of breading it and frying.
Preheat oven to 350° F.

fillets of fish (flounder, etc.)
butter
salt, pepper, paprika
mayonnaise
sour cream
mushrooms, sliced

Grease shallow baking dish. Dot fish with butter after laying in dish. Sprinkle with seasoning. Mix mayonnaise and sour cream in 1:2 proportions. Make enough of this to cover the fish . . . we like to smother it! Bake for at least an hour, adding the mushrooms on top during the last 15 minutes.

From the University of North Carolina, Chapel Hill:

Patty's Jambalaya

1 large onion, finely chopped
2 tablespoons shortening or bacon drippings
2 tablespoons flour
1 lb. hot sausage, cut in 1″ slices
1 8-oz. can tomato sauce
1½ lbs. shrimp, preferably fresh (or 16-oz. can)
1 garlic clove, minced
½ bell pepper, chopped
3 tablespoons parsley
2 cups water
salt and pepper to taste

Sauté onion in shortening in heavy pot until translucent. Add flour and stir over medium-low heat until light brown.

Add sausage and shrimp and brown. Add tomato sauce, water, bell pepper, garlic, parsley, and salt and pepper. Cover and simmer for approximately 30 minutes.

To serve: Spoon over hot cooked rice.
Serves 8–10.

From the Curtis Institute of Music:

Tunafish Casserole

Preheat oven to 375° F.

1 package spaghetti
1 can tunafish, drained
2 cups peas (canned are all right)
½ cup onions, chopped
½ cup green peppers, chopped
2 tablespoons lemon juice
2 cups white sauce (made with light cream)
½ lb. mushrooms
½ teaspoon curry powder
1 teaspoon sherry

Boil spaghetti. When cooked, drain and put in casserole with crumbled tunafish. Add rest of the ingredients and mix all up. Cover and bake about 45 minutes. Serves 4.

From the University of Maryland:

Baked Herbed Fish

Preheat oven to 375° F.

1 package frozen spinach
3 tablespoons almonds, minced
1 lb. fish fillets
½ cup butter, melted
1 teaspoon or more tarragon
salt and pepper

Cook spinach as directed on package only with ½ the amount of water and a pat of butter. Drain but reserve cooking liquid.

Mix spinach with almonds and put on bottom of baking dish. Lay fish on top of spinach, and pour on melted butter which has been mixed with spinach liquid and tarragon. Salt and pepper to taste. Cover and bake 30–45 minutes.

Best served with little roast potatoes which can be roasted at the same time . . . or with very dry white rice. Serves 3–4.

From Mills College:

Salmon and Mushroom Casserole

Preheat oven to 375° F.

1 can salmon, drained
4 cups cooked brown rice
2 cups white sauce
1 lb. mushrooms, sliced
3 cups broccoli, chopped
½ cup cheddar cheese, diced
½ cup raisins, moist or soaked
**   5 minutes in hot water**

Throw it all in a greased casserole dish. Mix up with forks thoroughly. Cover and bake for about 45 minutes.

VEGETABLES

Recipes included and the main ingredients needed

GREEN BEANS IN TOMATO SAUCE
   Green beans, onion, tomato paste

THERESE'S SISTER'S GOURMET GREEN BEANS
   Green beans, mushrooms, almonds

TANGY GREEN BEANS
   Green beans, bacon, onion

SAUTÉED GREEN BEANS
   Green beans, sesame seeds

GREEN BEANS WITH SOUR CREAM
   Green beans, Swiss cheese, almonds,
   onion, sour cream

SCALLOPED VEGETABLES
   Potatoes, onions, assorted vegetables

VIENNESE CABBAGE CASSEROLE
   Cabbage, onion, sour cream, bacon fat

FRIED CHINESE CABBAGE
   Chinese cabbage

EGGPLANT PARMIGIANA
   Eggplant, mozzarella, tomato sauce

BROILED EGGPLANT
   Eggplant, tomato sauce

FRIED CUCUMBERS
   Cucumbers, eggs, cornmeal

RATATOUILLE
Eggplant, zucchini, tomatoes, onion

SUE'S STUFFED MUSHROOMS
Mushrooms, celery, onions

SPINACH PUDDING
Spinach, milk, eggs

SPINACH-AND-MUSHROOM CASSEROLE
Spinach, mushrooms, onion, white sauce

POTATO PANCAKE
Potatoes, eggs, onions

SPINACH WITH SOUR CREAM
Spinach, sour cream

BAKED CARROTS AND YAMS
Yams, carrots, eggs, milk

QUICK-FRY VEGETABLES
Fresh mixed vegetables

QUICK-AND-EASY CASSEROLE
Zucchini or eggplant, tomatoes, green peppers, onions, sharp cheese, cashews or almonds

ZUCCHINI-TOMATO QUICKIE
Zucchini, tomatoes, onion

SHREDDED ZUCCHINI
Zucchini

ORANGE-YAM CASSEROLE
Yams, oranges, orange juice, sherry

VELVET YAMS
Yams

LEFT-OVER (OR NOT) BAKED YAMS
Yams

ZINGY CARROTS
Carrots, lemon juice, oregano, garlic, black olives

Vegetables are cheap, tasty, and provide a welcome variety to the menu. Some are very versatile, almost all can be eaten both raw and cooked. The simplest way of preparing a vegetable . . . boiled in as little water as possible, and served with butter and salt . . . can't be beat. But there are many other good ways and students sent me more vegetable recipes than any other kind. Since many of them are vegetarians, they have gone to a lot of trouble to make their meals interesting. If you have a favorite that is not included, I'd very much like to hear about it. Students seem to be vegetarians for one of two reasons . . . some through conviction, some because meat is too expensive for their budget. The lower cost of a vegetarian diet is a big advantage . . . if you are careful, you can eat almost as well as a meat-eater for a lot less. However, I, for one, would miss meat very much. Vegetarians have one big disadvantage . . . the problem of getting sufficient complete protein in their diet. Eggs added to vegetable and pasta dishes are a satisfactory meat substitute; soybeans, all dried beans, cheese, nuts, and milk all add valuable protein of various kinds . . . but you have to know what you are doing or you will gradually lose energy and health. A food may contain protein but not the right kind. So you have to be really up on nutrition . . . on the different kinds of protein, how much of each the body requires, etc. If you are a vegetarian, plan your food intake carefully. If you just assume that all vegetables are good for you and it doesn't matter what combination of them you eat, you will find yourself in trouble. The effects of an unbalanced diet can be slow; you may not realize what is happening right away.

Most of these vegetable dishes are quick and easy. However, be sure to add preparation time (for peeling, chopping, etc.) to cooking time when you are making your meal plans. In "Shredded Zucchini," for instance, it takes as long to shred the zucchini as to cook it.

From Vassar College:

Green Beans in Tomato Sauce

butter or oil
1 onion, diced
2 cups water
1 beef bouillon cube
½ teaspoon salt
¼ teaspoon pepper
¼ teaspoon cinnamon
½ teaspoon garlic salt
1 lb. green beans, cut in 1″ pieces
4 oz. tomato paste

Heat butter or oil in saucepan and brown onions. Add water and bring to a boil. Add bouillon cube and seasoning. Stir. Add beans and tomato paste. Stir till thoroughly mixed. Simmer ½ hour. Serves 6.

From the University of Colorado:

Therese's Sister's Gourmet Green Beans

1 lb. fresh or frozen green beans
½ cup mushrooms, sliced
2 tablespoons almonds, slivered
2 tablespoons oil
½ teaspoon thyme
¼ teaspoon sage

Sauté beans, mushrooms and almonds in hot oil. Add seasoning and toss. (Cook until beans are crisp-tender.) Douse with grated cheese, gush it all together. Serve hot. Serves 4.

From the University of Colorado:

Tangy Green Beans

1 lb. green beans, cut up
2 slices bacon, diced
½ onion, minced
¼ cup vinegar
salt and pepper to taste

Cook beans in boiling, salted water for 20 minutes.

Meanwhile, fry bacon until crisp. Take out bacon and sauté onion in bacon fat until golden. Add bacon and vinegar. Heat to boiling. When beans are done, pour bacon and sauce over beans, season and toss. Serves 4–5.

From Goddard College:

Sautéed Green Beans

2 tablespoons olive oil or butter
1 lb. green beans, in 1″ pieces
1 garlic clove, minced
1 teaspoon sesame seeds
¼ teaspoon nutmeg

Heat butter or oil in skillet until it sizzles when bean is dropped into it. Add all ingredients and toss lightly to coat them with butter or oil. Cook, tossing lightly from time to time, until desired consistency (5–10 minutes). You can cook them to crisp, stir-fried consistency like Chinese vegetables, or until tender, like American vegetables. Taste as you go along and see at what point they suit you. Serves 5–6.

From the University of Denver:

Green Beans with Sour Cream

We love this way of cooking beans. I suggest you prepare the vegetables and put them in the casserole before you make the sauce. Any kind of cheese and any nuts you like are o.k.

Preheat oven to 400° F.

1 onion, minced
2 lbs. Frenched green beans, cooked
1 teaspoon sugar
2 tablespoons butter
1 tablespoon flour
1 teaspoon salt
½ teaspoon pepper
½ pint sour cream
2 tablespoons Swiss cheese, grated
2 tablespoons almonds, chopped

Mix onions, beans, and sugar and put in buttered casserole. Melt butter in pan until foamy. Take off burner and stir in flour, adding gradually. Put back on burner for one minute, stirring occasionally. Add salt, pepper, sour cream, and heat but do not boil. Spoon sauce over vegetables and toss lightly until it is all mixed up. Sprinkle with grated cheese and almonds. Bake for 15–20 minutes.

From Boston University:

Scalloped Vegetables

You can use just potatoes and onions, if that's all there is. Amount of ingredients are approximate, so long as you use enough potatoes.
   Preheat oven to 350° F.

3 cups potatoes, sliced
whole-wheat flour
6 carrots, sliced
6 onions, sliced
3 stalks celery, chopped
3 green onions, chopped
1½ to 3 cups milk
1 teaspoon salt
1 teaspoon paprika

Dredge potatoes in flour. Arrange vegetables in layers, with potatoes forming every other layer. A low casserole or round baking dish is good. Dot layers with butter as you go along. Heat milk with seasonings and pour over vegetables. Bake covered 30 minutes; if you don't have a cover, use foil. Then uncovered for another ½ to ¾ hour, until vegetables are tender and all milk is fairly thickened and absorbed. Serves 6.

From the University of Maine:

Viennese Cabbage Casserole

Preheat oven to 350° F.

9 cups cabbage, shredded
¼ cup bacon fat
2 tablespoons onion, finely chopped
1 cup sour cream
2 teaspoons salt
2 teaspoons paprika

Sauté cabbage in hot bacon fat 5 minutes. Add onion and seasoning. Put in 1 qt. casserole and spoon sour cream over the top. Bake for 30 minutes. Serves 6.

From the University of Denver:

Fried Chinese Cabbage

1 Chinese cabbage
1 garlic clove, minced
2 tablespoons olive oil
salt, pepper to taste

Wash cabbage and shake thoroughly dry. It's even better to wash it in the morning and stand it upside down to drain. Then cook it in the afternoon when you are hungry. Cut off bottom of cabbage and chop the rest up coarsely. Sauté garlic lightly in hot oil. Add cabbage and toss for 8 to 10 minutes. Season. Serves 3–4.

From Columbia University:

Eggplant Parmigiana

Preheat oven to 325° F.

1 eggplant, cut in 1″ slices
2 cups bread crumbs
3 tablespoons olive oil
2 garlic cloves, minced
1 small can tomato sauce
1 cup mozzarella cheese, diced
3 tablespoons grated Parmesan cheese

Bread eggplant and fry in hot olive oil with garlic. Place in flat pan. Pour tomato sauce over eggplant and dot with mozzarella. Bake for 30 minutes. Five minutes before it is done, sprinkle with Parmesan cheese and put under broiler until cheese is melted.

From Columbia University:

Broiled Eggplant

Preheat broiler.

1 eggplant, cut in ½" thick slices
1 can tomato sauce
1 teaspoon basil
1 teaspoon oregano
salt, pepper to taste

Involves simply shoving in broiler, cooking 5 minutes, turning, pouring on sauce (mixed with spices and seasoning), and broiling another 5–10 minutes. Leave skin on the eggplant . . . it's healthy.

From the University of New Mexico:

Fried Cucumbers

If you're looking for a different-tasting vegetable, try this one.

6 cucumbers, sliced
2 eggs, beaten
1½ cups cornmeal
4 tablespoons butter
salt and pepper to taste
sour cream or yogurt

Put cucumbers on paper toweling as you slice them. Pat tops dry, then dip both sides in beaten egg, then in cornmeal. Fry quickly in hot butter until brown, turning once.

Drain on paper towels, if necessary, and serve with sour cream or yogurt on the side.

From Prescott College:

Ratatouille

Preheat oven to 300° F.

1 medium-sized eggplant
3 zucchini
3 firm tomatoes
1 large onion
4–6 tablespoons olive oil
3 cloves garlic, minced
½ teaspoon oregano
vegetable salt to taste
grated Parmesan cheese

Peel and cut both eggplant and zucchini into 1½″ cubes. Chop tomatoes coarsely. Slice onion. Pour oil into large skillet; when hot, sauté zucchini and eggplant until lightly brown. Remove from pan. Lower heat and add onions, tomatoes, garlic, and seasoning. Simmer until onions are limp. Place all ingredients in casserole, sprinkle with cheese, cover and bake for 1 hour. Serve hot the first time, cold the next.

From the University of New Hampshire:

Sue's Stuffed Mushrooms

It looks complicated when you write it all out but it's very quick to do!

Preheat oven to 350° F.

1 lb. whole, fresh mushrooms
2½ tablespoons butter
1 slice stale bread or 1 cup plain croutons
½ stalk celery, chopped
¼ cup onions, chopped
salt, pepper to taste

Wipe mushroom caps with damp paper towel. Twist off stems. Scoop out gills (underside of mushroom cap) with a small spoon . . . an iced tea spoon works pretty well. Heat ½ tablespoon butter in skillet. Lay scooped out mushroom caps upside down in skillet; brown until juice rises in each cap. Remove and keep hot. Chop up mushroom stems. Mix bread, celery, onions, mushroom stems, and scooped-out gills. Add salt and pepper. Add remaining butter to skillet and heat. Put bread mixture in skillet, stir and heat thoroughly. Fill mushroom caps with heated bread mixture and bake 10 minutes.

One pound usually serves 2 as a main dish. The tiny ones don't stuff well. Can also be used as a hors d'oeuvre.

From Vassar College:

Spinach Pudding

Preheat oven to 350° F.

2 10-oz. package frozen chopped spinach
2 tablespoons butter
¼ cup all-purpose flour
¾ cup milk
2 teaspoons salt
½ teaspoon pepper
¼ – ½ teaspoon nutmeg
3 eggs, beaten

Cook spinach as directed on package but without adding water. Drain thoroughly. Melt butter in a heavy pan; add flour, stirring constantly. Stir in milk gradually; add seasonings and spinach. Stir in beaten egg. Spinach should be well mixed and well coated with everything. Turn into greased 1½ qt. casserole. Place in pan of hot water and bake for 30 minutes. Serve right from casserole, or unmold and serve on warm plate with hot heavy cream (optional). Serves 6–8.

From Vassar College:

Spinach-and-Mushroom Casserole

Preheat oven to 325° F.

2 lbs. spinach, fresh, or 2 packages, frozen
3 tablespoons onion, grated
1 lb. mushrooms (caps and stems) sliced
4 tablespoons grated Swiss cheese
2½ cups white sauce

If spinach is fresh, wash thoroughly to remove sand. Allow plenty of time for this. Drain well and chop coarsely. Or thaw frozen spinach and drain well. Arrange spinach, onions, and mushrooms in alternate layers, starting with spinach. Add sauce each three layers, ending with a topping of sauce. Sprinkle with cheese and bake for 45 minutes.

From the Curtis Institute of Music:

Potato Pancake

3 potatoes, grated
¾ cup onions, chopped
2 eggs
1 teaspoon oil
salt, pepper to taste

Mix potatoes and onions together and add 2 beaten-up eggs. Blend well. Pour into *small* skillet, well-greased and hot. To brown, quick-fry at high heat on both sides. Then put under broiler for 10 minutes. Season to taste. Serves 2.

From the University of Louisville:

Spinach with Sour Cream

Preheat oven to 350° F.

1½ **cups sour cream**
1 **tablespoon onion salt**
1 **garlic clove, minced**
2 **packages frozen chopped spinach, cooked and drained until very dry**
1 **cup bread crumbs**
4 **tablespoons sherry**
½ **teaspoon ginger**
salt and pepper

Put sour cream, onion salt, and garlic in blender and blend. Or mix very, very thoroughly with fork. Add to all the other ingredients and mix thoroughly. Put in casserole, top with bread crumbs. Bake 25 minutes.

From the University of California at Los Angeles:

Baked Carrots and Yams

Preheat oven to 300° F.

1½ lb. carrots
1 lb. yams
4 medium eggs
1 cup milk
3 tablespoons melted butter
½ stick safflower margarine

Peel and parboil carrots. Cook yams in their jackets, then peel them. Grate carrots and yams.

Beat eggs and milk in a mixing bowl, then add:

4 tablespoons brown sugar
1 teaspoon sea salt
¼ teaspoon ground cinnamon

Add shredded carrots and yams and mix well. Pour into baking dish lined with butter. Dot with margarine and bake for 30 minutes. Serves 6.

From Mills College:

Quick-Fry Vegetables

butter
chopped fresh mixed vegetables

If you have a *wok,* this is the perfect pan. Otherwise use a heavy frying pan. Heat about 2 tablespoons of butter. Add bean sprouts, onions, green peppers, mushrooms, string beans, asparagus, broccoli, cauliflower, escarole, water chestnuts, hearts of palm . . . or any combination that appeals to you. For the last 30–60 seconds, add fresh spinach thoroughly washed and drained.

All vegetables should be chopped or thinly sliced so they will cook fast. Cook only a few minutes until hot all the way through. Taste to be sure. Serve as is with seasoning or make sauce as follows:

Sauce: Just before serving, add 3 tablespoons soy sauce and a little cornstarch mixed to a paste in cold water. Cook a minute more until sauce gets thick and transparent. If it gets too thick, add a little water or chicken broth; too thin, add more cornstarch. Don't worry if it doesn't come out exactly right the first try. Serve over hot rice or noodles.

From the University of California at Los Angeles:

Quick-and-Easy Casserole

Preheat oven to 375° F. In any large casserole, slice and aesthetically arrange:

4 zucchini or one small eggplant
4 tomatoes
2 green peppers
2 onions
1 lb. sharp cheese, grated
cashews or almonds, chopped
small pieces of bread (optional)

Bake for 45 minutes. Serve with rice.

From the University of Denver:

Zucchini-Tomato Quickie

1 large onion, sliced
2 tomatoes, chopped
4-5 medium zucchini, sliced but not peeled
1 teaspoon oregano
salt to taste

Heat butter in a large saucepan. Put in onion and cook until limp. Add tomato and zucchini. Season. Cover pan and cook, stirring occasionally, till zucchini is tender but not soggy. No water needed— the zucchini has enough water in it.

You can make this a main dish by browning a pound of hamburger with the onions and then making everything else according to the rest of the recipe.

From William Smith College:

Shredded Zucchini

Very, very quick and good!

3–4 small zucchini
2 tablespoons butter or olive oil
sait, pepper

Grate zucchini on coarse side of grater. Cook in hot butter or oil for about 3 minutes, tossing the whole time. Season with salt and freshly ground pepper.

You can do the same thing with shredded carrots . . . add ½ teaspoon of ginger or 1 teaspoon poppy or caraway seeds.

From Williams College:

Orange-Yam Casserole

This makes a special company dish . . . good with baked ham or chicken.
   Preheat oven to 350° F.

8 yams
¾ cup melted butter
½ cup sherry
1 cup orange juice
1 tablespoon orange rind, grated
salt, pepper
½ cup honey
3 oranges peeled and divided into segments
¼ cup brown sugar

Put whole, unpeeled yams into large pan of boiling salted water. Boil until fork pierces easily into center . . . about 30 minutes depending on size of yams. Peel and mash yams in large bowl with almost all of the butter, sherry, orange juice, orange rind. Add seasoning and drizzle in honey, stirring to get it all through. Put in buttered casserole and arrange orange segments decoratively on top. Dissolve brown sugar in rest of orange juice, add sherry and rind and sprinkle over oranges. Bake for 30 minutes and serve hot. Heats up easily for another night. Serves 6–8.

From Prescott College:

Velvet Yams

Really, really good. Really, really simple.

Yams—the fat red velvet ones are best—baked in foil. Spread with butter first . . . then bake in 375° F. oven,
> wood stove,
>> fireplace, or
>>> campfire.

Serve with salt and whipped sweet butter.

From Prescott College:

Leftover (or not) Baked Yams

If you have some baked yams left over, or even if not, make this with cooked yams.

Slice the yams, fry them as patties in hot butter. Then, when brown on both sides, serve with honey, molasses, brown sugar, maple syrup, or whatever . . . and a dash of nutmeg, cinnamon, or mace. Ginger is good too.

From Indiana University:

Zingy Carrots

Everyone likes carrots this way.

8 carrots, scraped and sliced
2 tablespoons olive oil
2 tablespoons lemon juice
1 teaspoon grated lemon rind
¼ teaspoon oregano
1 garlic clove, minced
½ cup black olives, chopped
salt to taste

Cook carrots until crisp-tender, about 10 minutes. Combine other ingredients in small saucepan and heat to boiling. When carrots are done, drain and pour sauce over them.

This recipe works hot or cold.

RICE AND PASTA

Recipes included and the main ingredients needed

BASIC BROWN RICE AND VEGETABLES
Brown rice, soy sauce, mixed fresh vegetables

YELLOW RICE
Rice, chicken broth, butter, saffron or curry or turmeric

FRIED RICE
Rice, eggs, scallions or onions, bean sprouts, ham, soy sauce

BROWN RICE PATTIES
Brown rice, carrots, onion, eggs, whole wheat flour

CLAM SPAGHETTI
Spaghetti, clams, butter, wine (optional), lemon juice, Parmesan cheese

SPAGHETTI ALLA CARBONARA
Spaghetti, eggs, Romano cheese, Parmesan cheese, bacon

SPAGHETTI WITH HOMEMADE MEAT SAUCE
Spaghetti, tomato sauce, tomato paste, ground beef, onion, garlic, parsley

KIM'S LASAGNA

Ground beef, mozzarella cheese, lasagna noodles, garlic, tomato paste, onion, parsley, cottage cheese, Parmesan cheese, eggs

SAVORY RICE

Brown or white rice and one of the following: mushrooms; pine nuts; pineapple; pimientos, peas, ham and chicken; parsley and onion

JODI'S LASAGNA

Lasagna noodles, ground beef, ricotta or cottage cheese, onions, green pepper (optional), garlic, tomato sauce, mozzarella

SUPER-QUICK MACARONI AND CHEESE

Macaroni, American or similar cheese, milk

Rice and pasta dishes are very useful, inexpensive, and substitute interestingly for potatoes. They are especially indispensable for those days when the budget is low . . . because the amount of meat, vegetables, or cheese used is flexible; you can add more or less depending on what you can afford. Because of this flexibility, most of these recipes are foolproof . . . almost any proportion of main ingredients tastes good as long as you have enough sauce. If you misjudged and need more sauce in a hurry, add more olive oil or butter, whichever the recipe calls for, and toss thoroughly. In substituting brown for white rice, see the table of substitutions. In general, you will need to use more water and allow a longer cooking time.

From the University of California at Los Angeles:

Basic Brown Rice and Vegetables

Preheat oven to 350° F.

4 cups raw brown rice
6 cups water
2 tablespoons soy sauce

Mix together and bake for 1½ hours, covered. This gives you your basic rice and it will come out with a fuller, nuttier flavor and dryer texture than boiled rice.

To cook vegetables: Sauté in 2 tablespoons of butter or oil any combination of chopped up vegetables such as scallions, bean sprouts, alfalfa sprouts, zucchini, green peppers, tomato, green beans, carrots, celery, etc. Do not sauté vegetables more than 5 minutes or they will lose their crispness. Add a bit of soy sauce to the pan at the last minute to enrich the sauce; serve over rice. Don't salt this until you taste it . . . the soy should be enough. May be garnished with grated jack cheese or even yogurt. Grated nuts . . . almonds or cashews . . . add protein and variety.

From Rice University:

Yellow Rice

This is fabulous with broiled chicken. We make it three ways by varying the seasoning. Each seasoning has its own color and taste, so you'll have to try them all to see which one you like best.

2 tablespoons butter
1 teaspoon salt
½ teaspoon pepper
¼ teaspoon saffron *or* **2 tablespoons curry** *or*
**   2 tablespoons turmeric**
1 cup rice
2 cups hot chicken broth

Melt butter in pan and add seasoning. Stir to blend. Add rice and stir to coat with butter and seasoning. Cook five minutes, stirring occasionally so rice does not stick or burn. Add hot chicken broth; stir well once. Cover tightly and cook without looking on *low heat* for 25 minutes. Liquid should be completely absorbed and rice should be golden and tender.

From the University of Denver:

Fried Rice

No matter how broke you are, vary your meals. If you're serving an ordinary meal to your boyfriend, put candles on the table. . . it makes it more special.

4 cups rice, cooked
⅓ cup oil (peanut oil is traditional)
2 eggs
3 tablespoons soy sauce
½ cup scallions or onion, minced
½ cup bean sprouts
½ cup ham, chopped

Left-over rice is fine. Sauté cooked rice in oil until lightly browned. Keep stirring—don't let it stick on the bottom of the pan if you can help it. Add eggs and soy sauce and cook, stirring until eggs are solid and all broken up in among the rice. Add other ingredients and cook until everything is hot . . . not very long. Serves 4.

From the University of California at Irvine:

Brown Rice Patties

8 cups cooked brown rice
½ cup parsley, minced
1 cup carrots, grated
½ cup onion, minced
1 clove garlic, minced
1 teaspoon salt
2 eggs, beaten
½ cup whole wheat flour
1 cup oil (sesame is especially tasty)

Combine all ingredients except oil, mixing well.
Form into patties, pressing firmly with hands and
making uniform in size so they will all be ready at
the same time. You won't be able to get all of them
in one skillet, so keep the first ones hot by covering
them with foil or placing them in a warm oven (if
you have one).

Heat oil in skillet and fry patties until brown on
both sides (you should turn them only once).

Makes 12 patties.

Note: If you don't have brown rice, only white,
add chopped peanuts (about ½ cup) to make more
flavorful.

From Vassar College:

Clam Spaghetti

Whole meal takes 15 minutes to make . . . and it's a company dish!

spaghetti (sauce is for 1 package
   but you can make more)
1 stick butter
1 can minced clams
2 tablespoons parsley, dried or fresh, minced
2 tablespoons onion salt
1 teaspoon garlic powder
grated Parmesan cheese
½ teaspoon black pepper
½ teaspoon salt
¼ cup white wine or vermouth (optional)
2 teaspoons lemon juice

Put spaghetti into boiling salted water and cook until done.

Melt butter in small saucepan and add the clam juice drained from the can of clams. Add parsley, onion salt, garlic, pepper, salt. Cook on very low heat. Five minutes before spaghetti is ready, add wine and lemon juice and clams. Drain spaghetti. Put cheese on bottom of individual bowls and place spaghetti over it. Then spoon sauce over each serving. Sauce is for 4 people.

Spaghetti alla Carbonara

We would rather eat home than in the college cafeteria because we like to eat food that has been prepared by people who care about what they are eating and what they are creating.

spaghetti
bacon
eggs
Romano cheese, grated
Parmesan cheese, grated
salt and pepper

Cook and drain spaghetti.

While spaghetti is cooking: Sauté bacon until crisp, then combine with a little olive oil . . . do not drain off bacon fat. Separate yolks and whites of eggs. Use one egg for each person you are planning to serve. Beat yolks and add a little of the whites . . . less than half of what you have. Grate lots of cheese into the eggs and add pepper till everything is black.

When spaghetti is cooked and drained, add beaten eggs and bacon and toss. Top with more grated cheese when serving.

From Vassar College:

Spaghetti with Homemade Meat Sauce

Make sauce first. It takes longer and it doesn't matter if it simmers lots more than an hour. This is a very meaty sauce . . . practically a meal in itself. You could use half as much meat if you needed to.

1 **medium onion, diced**
2 **tablespoons olive oil**
1 **lb. ground hamburger**
12 **oz. can tomato paste**
24 **oz. can tomato sauce**
2 **cloves garlic, pressed**
3 **tablespoons parsley, minced**
1 **teaspoon oregano**
1 **teaspoon salt**
½ **teaspoon pepper**
1 **teaspoon basil**
1 **package of spaghetti**

Sauté onion in olive oil. When onions turn translucent, brown meat in olive oil–onion mixture. Add rest of ingredients (except spaghetti) and simmer for 1 hour, at least.

Cook and drain spaghetti and serve with sauce and grated cheese. Serves 6.

From Texas Christian University:

Kim's Lasagna

This is one of my very favorite recipes. It makes up one meal to which we are certain to have guests . . . who "just happen to be in the neighborhood." All of our friends love it. *One caution:* let the lasagna stand at least 10 minutes before cutting or you may wind up snipping stringy cheese with the scissors (as we did!).

Preheat oven to 375° F.

1 lb. ground beef
1 garlic clove, minced
1 tablespoon basil
1½ teaspoons salt
2 6-oz. cans tomato paste
½ cup onion, minced
snipped fresh parsley or parsley flakes
10 oz. lasagna noodles
1 lb. mozzarella cheese, sliced thin

Cheese filling:
3 cups creamy cottage cheese
½ cup Parmesan, grated
2 tablespoons parsley flakes or fresh parsley
2 beaten eggs
2 teaspoons salt
½ teaspoon pepper

Brown meat. Add all other ingredients, except cheese filling, to meat. Simmer ½ hour, stirring occasionally. Cook lasagna noodles until tender.

Mix cheese filling ingredients well. In large baking dish, put a layer of ½ of noodles, ½ cheese filling, ½ mozzarella, ½ meat sauce. Repeat each layer. Bake for 30 minutes. Let stand 10 minutes before cutting. Serves 12.

From the University of Texas:

Savory Rice

Use either brown or white rice, depending on your preference. Cook as you usually do (or follow directions on package). When done, add to the hot cooked rice any one of the following:

sautéed sliced mushrooms
pine nuts
minced pineapple and mint flakes
minced pimientos and cooked peas, heated with bits of cooked ham or chicken or both and bit of tarragon
minced parsley and minced onions

Toss well and serve. This is so cheap you can even have it for lunch.

From Goddard College:

Jodi's Lasagna

I use a lot of sauce; I find the more the better. If you make too much, it can always be frozen. Allow time for the sauce to simmer for an hour or longer.
  Preheat oven to 350°F.

2 15-oz. cans tomato sauce
1 or 2 onions, chopped
1 green pepper, chopped (optional)
1 garlic clove, minced
1 teaspoon oregano
1 teaspoon cinnamon
1 teaspoon sugar
1½ lbs. ground beef
1 small package lasagna noodles
2 lbs. ricotta or cottage cheese
24 oz. mozzarella cheese, sliced

Combine tomato sauce with onions, green pepper, garlic, oregano, cinnamon, and sugar. Simmer an hour or longer. Add meat after first ½ hour.
  Meanwhile boil lasagna noodles until just barely tender. In a greased 9" x 13" baking pan, place a layer of noodles, a layer of sauce, a layer of ricotta or cottage cheese. Add one more layer of noodles, cover with sauce and place thin slices of mozzarella all over top. Bake for 45 minutes or until cheese melts. Serves about 8–10 people.

From the University of Colorado:

Super-Quick Macaroni and Cheese

No baking—takes about 15 minutes.

Cook macaroni and drain well. Cut up American or any soft cheese into ¼" cubes. Add to hot noodles, stir until just melted. Add hot milk until desired consistency and "juicy" enough. Add salt, pepper, and butter (very important) to taste. Serve!

SALADS

Recipes included and the main ingredients needed

BEAN SALAD
Red kidney beans, white kidney beans, green beans, lima beans

HOT POTATO SALAD
Potatoes, bacon, onion, parsley

CHILLED POTATO SALAD
Potatoes, celery, green pepper, pimientos (optional), scallions, eggs, sweet pickles

COLESLAW
Cabbage, carrots, dill, celery seed, sweet pickles

LYNN'S COLESLAW
Cabbage, carrot, green pepper, zucchini

GUACAMOLE
Avocados, onion, tomato, lemon juice

CHEF'S SALAD
Ham, chicken, eggs (optional), cheese, salad greens or spinach

ORANGE-ONION SALAD
Oranges, onions, lettuce

TOBOULI
Parsley, bulgur, scallions, tomatoes, lemon or orange juice

POTATO SALAD WITH YOGURT
Potatoes, yogurt, carrots, cucumbers

214

INSPIRATION SALAD
A combination of leftovers . . . whatever you have on hand that inspires you

Americans are thought of as subsisting primarily on a diet of "meat-and-potatoes." While it is true that we eat a higher proportion of meat per capita than other countries, vegetables and salads are beginning to represent a much larger part of our menu. The French have always considered a mixed green salad the height of high cuisine, but we usually like something more in a salad than just greens. When dips became popular, everyone discovered that almost all vegetables taste good raw; as we became more sophisticated about nutrition, we found that raw vegetables not only taste good, they are good for you. Of course, every thrifty housewife long ago discovered that last night's vegetables are good cold in today's salads, and mixed bean salads are so popular that they are now sold, already made, in cans. A good salad dressing is, however, very important. Fortunately, the really great dressings are simple to make. You can't beat olive oil and vinegar plus a little salt, pepper, and garlic. Sour cream forms the base of good dressings, as does yogurt, and if you want to take just a little more trouble, there is homemade mayonnaise . . . a far cry from the commercial product.

A salad can be a meal, a side dish, or a separate course . . . so adapt the quantities in the following recipes according to how you want to serve them.

From Rice University:

Bean Salad

1 cup *each* cooked: red kidney beans, white
   kidney beans, green beans, lima beans
1 onion, chopped
3 tablespoons olive oil
3 tablespoons vinegar
1 teaspoon sugar
½ teaspoon dry mustard
1 teaspoon salt
½ teaspoon fresh ground pepper

Make dressing and toss thoroughly. Refrigerate at
least 1 hour before serving.

From the University of Minnesota:

Hot Potato Salad

6 potatoes
4 slices bacon
1 onion, diced
1 tablespoon parsley, minced
⅓ cup vinegar
1 tablespoon sugar
1 teaspoon salt
½ teaspoon pepper

Cook potatoes in jackets. Peel and dice.

Meanwhile, fry bacon until crisp.

Mix parsley, vinegar, sugar, salt, pepper, heat to boiling point. Crumble bacon into hot potatoes. Add onions and vinegar mixture. Toss lightly until thoroughly mixed. Serve hot.

From the University of Louisville:

Chilled Potato Salad

Enough for a big picnic.

5 lbs. potatoes, cooked in jackets
½ cup celery, chopped
½ cup green pepper, chopped
small jar pimientos (optional), diced
6 scallions, diced
4-5 hard-cooked eggs, diced
1 cup mayonnaise
1 teaspoon prepared mustard
4-5 tablespoons pickle liquid
8 sweet pickles, diced

Pare and dice cooked potatoes while still hot. Add other ingredients. Mix thoroughly and add more mayonnaise, if needed. Refrigerate until chilled all through.

From the University of Denver:

Coleslaw

We have a saying, "coleslaw today . . . mushrooms tomorrow," because coleslaw is so easy on the budget. Easy on time too.

Grate half a head of cabbage, 2 carrots, add a little dill and a pinch of celery seed. Mince sweet pickles. Mix some pickle juice with mayonnaise to make the mayonnaise runny and tangy. Toss everything together.

From the University of Colorado:

Lynn's Coleslaw

A little change from the usual coleslaw.

¼ head cabbage, shredded
1 carrot, shredded
1 green pepper, shredded
1 zucchini, shredded
½ cup mayonnaise
salt, pepper to taste

Mix all together. Add more mayonnaise if necessary. Very, very good on a ham or corned beef sandwich instead of lettuce.

From Williams College:

Guacamole

Like all Mexican food, this is good and easy. And if avocado is the "poor man's butter" as they say in Caribbean islands, it sure takes some of the sting out of being poor.

2 ripe avocados
2 tablespoons onion, chopped
1 tomato, chopped
1 tablespoon lemon juice
hot sauce or chili to taste
salt and pepper to taste

Just mush all up and serve on leafy salad greens or as a dip.

From the University of Denver:

Chef's Salad

Easy to make.

Chop up or sliver cooked ham, chicken, hard-cooked eggs (optional), Swiss or American cheese . . . a little crisp bacon tastes good too. Mix it all up with whatever greens you have handy— spinach is fine. Add dressing and toss.

From New York University:

Orange-Onion Salad

1 **tablespoon oil**
1 **tablespoon vinegar**
1 **teaspoon salt**
¼ **teaspoon pepper**
¼ **teaspoon sugar**
1 **head lettuce**
2 **oranges, peeled and sliced**
2 **onions, sliced**

Mix oil, vinegar, salt, pepper, and sugar.

Wash lettuce and put on plate, forming a comparatively flat surface. Arrange orange and onion slices alternately on lettuce. Pour dressing over it all just before serving.

Another way is to chop up oranges, onions, and tear lettuce into small pieces. Then toss with dressing and serve in small bowls.

From Prescott College:

Tobouli

Very, very good—refreshing. Bulgur keeps better, both cooked and uncooked, than any other grain. Our garden is organic, so we have lots of parsley practically free . . . you can even grow it on the windowsill in a dorm.

6 bunches parsley, chopped
3 cups cooked or soaked bulgur
2 bunches of scallions, finely chopped
3-4 tomatoes, chopped
4 tablespoons olive oil
salt to taste
¾-1 cup lemon or orange juice

Mix well, chill. Eat cold.

From the University of New Mexico:

Potato Salad with Yogurt

Easy, filling, and a little different.

6 potatoes, cooked and sliced
1 cup yogurt
1 tablespoon vinegar
½ cup raw carrots, shredded (optional)
½ cup cucumbers, chopped (optional)
salt and pepper to taste

Stir gently to combine all ingredients except potatoes. Toss potatoes gently with yogurt mixture and serve.

From Hobart College:

Inspiration Salad

The fun about this is that it's different every time.

If you carefully save leftovers, the way we do, you end up with a couple of spoonfuls of green beans, carrots, pineapple chunks, old mushrooms, raw turnip, ham, chicken, bean sprouts, rice, hard-cooked eggs, cold potatoes, cheese, bulgur, olives, etc.

Cut up everything you want to get rid of *very, very* small. Mix with a slightly vinegary dressing . . . it works better if you have an oil like olive oil that has a lot of flavor . . . add a minced garlic clove, some minced sweet onion. Toss until everything is thoroughly mixed with the dressing. Serve on crisp salad greens. It's delicious and everything goes together beautifully.

SAUCES, GRAVIES, AND SALAD DRESSINGS

Recipes included and the main ingredients needed

BUTTER SAUCE
Butter

LEMON BUTTER SAUCE
Butter, lemon juice

CURRY SAUCE (BUTTER)
Butter, curry powder or curry spices

CLAM SAUCE (BUTTER)
Butter, chopped clams, garlic

ONION SAUCE (BUTTER)
Butter, onions

WHITE SAUCE
Butter, flour, milk or stock

BROWN SAUCE OR GRAVY
Butter, flour, pan drippings or stock

CURRY SAUCE
White or brown sauce, curry powder

MUSHROOM SAUCE
White or brown sauce, mushrooms

ONION SAUCE
White or brown sauce, onions

CHEESE SAUCE
White or brown sauce, grated cheese

SOUR-CREAM SALAD DRESSING
Sour cream, vinegar

FINEST SALAD DRESSING
Cider vinegar, safflower oil, paprika, basil, and other spices

SALAD DRESSING II
Olive oil, cider or wine vinegar, garlic

WINE MARINADE
Oil, soy sauce, Worcestershire sauce, mustard, wine, parsley flakes, lemon juice

GERMAN SALAD DRESSING
Cider vinegar, sugar

Sauces, gravies, and salad dressings are used to add moisture and flavor to the foods they accompany. Most of them are very easy to make in spite of the fact that cookbooks often give them fancy names. They are essential if you want to make the most of leftovers, turning them into delicious meals. Sauces you make yourself save you the extra expense of canned gravies and "convenience" foods; and they provide better nutrition because they do not contain the additives, "flavor enhancers," and other chemicals of commercial products. Easy, inexpensive, healthier . . . these simple basic recipes are an indispensable part of any cook's repetory.

From Columbia University:

Butter Sauces

If a recipe calls for "drawn" or melted butter, that's a butter sauce. It's very useful.

Lemon Butter Sauce: we use this for fish. It's just melted butter with salt, pepper, and lemon juice added.

Curry Sauce: if we don't have time to make a real curry sauce, we add curry spices (turmeric, etc.) to butter instead. Or, if you don't make your own curry, a tablespoon of ready-made curry powder to a cup of melted butter does the job.

Clam Sauce: Minced garlic cloves and as many chopped clams (canned are fine) as you feel like added to melted butter, with salt and pepper, is a good quick white clam sauce for spaghetti . . . very expensive in restaurants, very inexpensive at home.

Onion Sauce: Chop up onions and add them to melted butter. Brown or not, depending on the flavor you want.

We make lots of others but this should give you the idea. Lots of times we just add an herb . . . like tarragon for chicken, rosemary for lamb chops; this makes an herb butter for a broiled dish.

From the University of Pittsburgh:

White Sauce and Brown Sauce or Gravy

These are the two basic sauces . . . very, very simple. The proportions are what is important. . . . No matter how much or how little you want to make, always stick to these proportions (except for cheese sauce).

2 **tablespoons butter**
2 **tablespoons flour**
1 **cup of:**
   milk or stock for *white sauce* or
   pan drippings for *gravies*
seasoning to taste

Melt butter in saucepan. Blend in flour, cook 1 minute, stirring constantly. Add liquid gradually, still stirring constantly. Lower heat and cook until it thickens (a few minutes), stirring occasionally.

VARIATIONS:

Curry Sauce: Add a tablespoon of curry powder.

Mushroom Sauce: Sauté sliced mushrooms in butter a few minutes, before adding flour. If you want a really rich sauce, add heavy cream instead of milk.

Onion Sauce: Chop onions and brown in butter before adding flour and liquid.

Cheese Sauce: 2 tablespoons butter to 1 tablespoon of flour to 1 cup milk. Then add ¾ cup of grated American (or similar) cheese, and heat until it blends and melts into everything else. Stir pretty steadily all the time you are making this . . . it doesn't take long. Don't keep the heat too high . . . cheese shouldn't be cooked at very high heat.

All you have to remember is that milk or cream makes a white sauce. So does stock unless you brown the flour in a frying pan before you add it. Pan drippings make a brown sauce or gravy. After that you can add anything you want.

From Union College (Schenectady, N.Y.):

Sour - Cream Salad Dressing

You can make a tart sour-cream dressing by adding a couple of spoonfuls of vinegar and a little salt and pepper to ½ pint of sour cream. Mix well.

A variation on this is to add a tablespoon of mayonnaise as well.

Or you can make a dressing that's especially good with fruit salads by adding fruit juice instead of vinegar.

Two from Columbia University:

Finest Salad Dressing

My vinegar-and-oil salad dressing is the finest.

Cider vinegar and safflower oil . . . slightly more vinegar than oil. Heavy dashes of turmeric, paprika, fresh ground pepper, garlic and onion powder, curry, basil, thyme, celery seed . . . it should look red from the paprika, heavy on the basil. Balance it out to taste.

SALAD DRESSING II
But for purists, equal parts of olive oil and vinegar (cider or wine vinegar, preferably) . . . or slightly more oil than vinegar. Minced garlic, salt and pepper to taste.

From Vassar College:

Wine Marinade

I guess you would want to include a marinade in sauces . . . since it's really a basting sauce you soak something in before cooking. A marinade can be re-used if you have any left over . . . freeze if you're not going to use it again right away.

1½ **cups peanut or other cooking oil**
¾ **cup soy sauce**
2 **teaspoons Worcestershire sauce**
2 **teaspoons dry mustard**
1 **teaspoon fresh ground pepper**
1 **cup dry red wine (cheap wine is acceptable)**
2 **teaspoons dried parsley flakes**
⅓ **cup fresh lemon juice (reconstituted works, too)**

Combine all ingredients in a quart mason jar. With cover on tight, shake vigorously. Or use blender. Marinate meat for at least 3 hours . . . overnight is better.

From the University of Minnesota:

German Salad Dressing

This is also good for marinating cold vegetables, like very thinly sliced cucumbers.

½ **cup cold water**
¼ **cup cider vinegar**
1 **teaspoon salt**
¼ **teaspoon pepper**
2 **teaspoons sugar**

Blend everything together and chill. It sounds simple but it's good.

DESSERTS

Recipes included and the main ingredients needed

SNICKERS
Flour, butter, sugar, eggs, cream of tartar

FRUIT YOGURT
Plain yogurt, dried fruit

COLONIAL APPLE CUSTARD
Applesauce, eggs, butter

NEW ENGLAND CHEESE CAKE
Zwieback, butter, cream cheese, eggs, sour cream

YOGURT PIE FILLING
Pie crust, yogurt, raisins, eggs, honey

FRUIT COCKTAIL CAKE
Canned fruit cocktail, flour, eggs, nuts, evaporated milk, butter, sugar

BUTTERSCOTCH BROWNIES
Brown sugar, oil, eggs, soy grits, wheat germ, whole-wheat flour, walnuts, powdered milk

APPLESAUCE
Apples

DATE CANDY FUDGE
Sugar, dates, walnuts, milk, butter

GRANOLA COOKIES
Granola, flour, eggs, butter

RICE PUDDING
Milk, honey, butter, cooked rice, eggs, raisins

LEMON CHEESE PIE
Cream cheese, butter, egg, flour, milk, lemon

APPLE CRISP
Apples, butter, flour, sugar

CAROB PEANUT BUTTER GOO CANDY
Carob powder, peanut butter, milk, honey

YUM YUM CAKE
Flour, butter, raisins

CHOCOLATE-CHIP TOAST
Toast, cream cheese, chocolate chips

Dessert is something we are never too full to eat. It need be no more than a perfectly ripe peach or a wedge of melon; it may be a dish that is extra rich and gooey. If it's served with a little ceremony . . . like a fruit knife and a salt shaker . . . it's more company dessert than an apple grabbed from a bowlful and eaten on the run. But both are satisfactory desserts and add to the pleasure of the meal that preceded them. Most of the recipes that were sent me are easy and quick to make, and run the gamut from fruity to really rich. Several of them are like five recipes in one because they lend themselves to many variations.

From Texas Christian University:

Snickers

My specialty is the sweet department. As I remember it, I learned to bake in elementary school because I loved cookies and Mother, always busy with things besides baking, invariably let the bottoms of the cookies burn, then tried to get us to eat them by telling us charcoal was good for our teeth!

Preheat oven to 400° F.

1 cup butter
1½ cups sugar
2 eggs
2¾ cups flour
2 teaspoons cream of tartar
1 teaspoon soda
¼ teaspoon salt
2 tablespoons sugar mixed with
   2 tablespoons cinnamon

Cream butter and sugar with spoon. Add eggs. Add flour, cream of tartar, soda, and salt mixed together. Mix thoroughly. Shape dough into 1″ balls. Roll in cinnamon sugar. Place 2″ apart on ungreased baking sheet. Bake 8–10 minutes. These cookies puff up at first and then flatten out. Makes 6 dozen cookies.

From Barnard College:

Fruit Yogurt

Mix plain or vanilla yogurt with dried fruit that has been boiled a few minutes. Keep in a jar in the icebox—much better than the too-sweet gooey fruit yogurt you buy.

If you *like* sweeter yogurt, make it yourself from plain yogurt plus a couple of spoonfuls of preserve, jam, or canned fruit (with a little of the syrup). Lots cheaper and better tasting.

From Yale University:

Colonial Apple Custard

This is easy to make . . . can be eaten as a side dish with meat, or for dessert with a topping of light cream or yogurt . . . makes a great pick-me-up while studying late at night.

Preheat oven to 350° F.

1 tablespoon melted butter
1 cup applesauce
3 eggs, beaten
¼ teaspoon salt

Butter 4 custard cups. Combine remaining butter, applesauce, eggs, and salt. Pour into custard cups. Bake approximately ½ hour or until knife comes out clean. May be eaten hot or cold. Serves 4.

From the University of New Hampshire:

New England Cheese Cake

In three steps. It's easier to make than to read all through!

    Preheat oven to 375° F.

Crust:

1 package of Zwieback
¼ cup butter, melted
1½ teaspoons cinnamon
2 tablespoons sugar

Crush crackers into crumbs (I put them in a plastic bag and pound them with a knife handle). Add melted butter, cinnamon, and sugar. Mix all together and press into 9″ spring form pan.

Filling:

3 8-oz. packages of cream cheese
3 eggs
1 cup sugar
½ teaspoon vanilla

Let cream cheese really soften. Then cream in mixing bowl (an electric beater is quick if you have one). Add eggs one at a time and then add sugar and vanilla. Beat well. Pour into crust. Bake for 30 minutes.

Topping: While pie is baking, make topping.

1 pint sour cream
4 tablespoons sugar
1 teaspoon vanilla

Blend all together until well-mixed. When cake is done, take out of oven. Turn up oven to 500° F. Spread topping on top of cake and put back in oven for 10 minutes. Cool well before refrigerating. YUM!

From Prescott College:

Yogurt Pie Filling

Use any recipe you like for pie crust, or buy a frozen one. If you buy a frozen one, buy two and use one for the crust.

Preheat oven to 450° F.

2 eggs
1 cup yogurt
½-1 cup honey
1 cup chopped raisins
½ teaspoon cinnamon
¼ teaspoon nutmeg
¼ teaspoon allspice

Beat egg yolks. Add yogurt, honey, raisins, spices. Beat egg whites. Fold yogurt mixture into egg whites. Fill pie and top with crust. Bake for 10 minutes at 450° F. Turn oven down to 350° F. and bake for 30 minutes.

You can vary this by using other fruit and different sweetening.

From Texas Christian University:

Fruit Cocktail Cake

Preheat oven to 325° F.

1 16-oz. can fruit cocktail
   (use juice in cake)
2 cups flour
1½ cups sugar
2 teaspoons soda
2 eggs
pinch salt
⅔ cup brown sugar
½ cup chopped nuts

Sauce:
1 stick butter
1½ cups sugar
1 small can evaporated milk
fruit from can

Drain fruit juice from fruit cocktail. Mix flour, sugar, soda, eggs, salt, and juice all together. When well-mixed, pour in well-greased and floured flat pan. Put on top, ⅔ cup brown sugar and chopped nuts. Bake 45 minutes.

Meanwhile, bring sauce ingredients to a boil. When cake is done, punch holes in it and pour the sauce over it.

From Prescott College:

Butterscotch Brownies

Preheat oven to 375° F.

2 cups brown sugar
½ cup oil
2 large eggs, beaten
1 teaspoon vanilla
⅔ cup whole-wheat flour (plus some extra for nuts and pan)
½ cup powdered milk
½ teaspoon salt
2 teaspoons baking powder
½ cup soy grits (soaked in ½ cup hot water)
⅔ cup wheat germ
1 cup walnut meats

Combine sugar, oil, and eggs; mix well. Add vanilla. Add sifted flour, milk, salt, baking powder; mix. Add grits, wheat germ, walnut meats dredged in flour (so they won't sink). Bake in greased, floured pan for 25–30 minutes. Let cool 5 minutes before cutting into squares.

From the University of Colorado:

Applesauce

Peel apples. Cut up and put in pot . . . cover about ¾" high with water. Add sugar, cinnamon, clove (sparingly), nutmeg, a little ginger . . . all to taste. Cook until mushy or however you like.

Also very good with unpeeled apples but don't cook them as long, because all the peels fall off.

From Prescott College:

Date Candy Fudge

3 cups sugar (or whatever you use:
   ½ white sugar, ½ brown date sugar)
1 cup chopped fresh dates
1 cup milk (regular or ½ evaporated, or the best
   is to use mostly condensed milk)
1 pat of butter
1 cup chopped walnuts

Put all together, except nuts. Bring to boil. Boil 15–20 minutes until it reaches the soft-ball stage. Take off fire. Add nuts and beat till just about stiff. Pour out; let harden. Cut.

From the University of California at Los Angeles:

Granola Cookies

Preheat oven to 375° F.

1 cup sifted flour
½ teaspoon baking powder
¼ teaspoon baking soda
¼ teaspoon salt
½ cup butter, softened
1 cup dark brown sugar
1 egg
1 teaspoon vanilla
2½ cups granola
¼ cup raisins (optional)

Sift together flour, baking powder, soda, and salt. Beat butter and sugar till light and fluffy. Add egg, vanilla; beat well. Add dry ingredients and mix well. Drop by level tablespoons onto greased baking sheet. Bake 10–12 minutes or until lightly browned. Makes approximately 5 dozen cookies.

From the University of Pittsburgh:

Rice Pudding

This is a great and easy dessert for us rice-pudding fans.

Preheat oven to 325°F.

1⅓ **cups milk**
½ **teaspoon salt**
3½ **tablespoons honey**
1 **tablespoon soft butter**
1 **teaspoon vanilla**
2 **eggs**
2 **cups cooked rice**
¼ **cup raisins, previously softened in water**
¼ **teaspoon cinnamon**

Combine and beat well: milk, salt, honey, butter, vanilla, and eggs. Add rice, raisins, and cinnamon. Grease baking dish. Pour in mixture. Sprinkle a little more cinnamon on top and bake for 1 hour.

From Prescott College:

Lemon Cheese Pie

Preheat oven to 350° F.

1 tablespoon softened butter
1 cup raw sugar
3 8-oz. packages cream cheese
1 egg
2 tablespoons flour
⅔ cup milk
¼ cup lemon juice
2 tablespoons lemon rind, grated

Cream butter and sugar together with spoon. Add cream cheese and egg and mix well. Add milk, lemon juice, and rind. Heat but do not let boil. Pour hot mixture into unbaked crust made of crumbs (graham cracker, etc.) or coconut. Bake for 45 minutes. Chill thoroughly before serving.

From Boston University:

Apple Crisp

This is easy and *delishous!* Preheat oven to 350° F.

9 McIntosh apples, peeled and sliced
1 tablespoon cinnamon
½ stick butter, slightly softened
½ cup flour
½ cup sugar

Into a casserole or pan, slice the apples, sprinkling each layer generously with cinnamon.

In a bowl, cream together with a spoon: butter, flour, and sugar. Spoon evenly over apples. Bake about 40 minutes. Serve warm with whipped cream.

From Prescott College:

Carob Peanut Butter Goo Candy

Tastes for all the world as if it were made with chocolate . . . quick to mix up when everyone feels like eating candy. No cooking!

Mix up:
- 3 **tablespoons carob powder**
- 4 **tablespoons peanut butter**
- 2 **tablespoons milk**
- 4 **tablespoons honey**

Beat till creamy. Refrigerate. It will stay soft but it can be sort of cut with a knife. If you freeze it, it will get a little firmer.

To serve easily, shape it in small balls (about the size of large marbles) and roll in chopped nuts or coconut . . . not so sticky to handle.

From the University of Denver:

Yum Yum Cake

Also has been known to serve as almost a "Poor Man's Cake."
   Preheat oven to 325°F.

3 cups water
1 lb. raisins
1 scant teaspoon baking soda
½ cup butter
2 cups sugar (brown or white or mixed)
1 heaping teaspoon cinnamon
1 scant teaspoon cloves
1 teaspoon nutmeg
4 cups flour, sifted

Pour 2 cups water over raisins and simmer 15 minutes. Take off fire, add 1 cup cold water, baking soda, butter, sugar, cinnamon, cloves, nutmeg, and flour. Mix in order given, adding sifted flour and spices last. Put in 10″ to 14″ pan and bake 1 to 1¼ hours.

From Prescott College:

Chocolate Chip Toast

Make toast. Spread with cream cheese . . . thickly. Sprinkle with chocolate chips.

Things to Eat When You Have to Stay Up All Night Studying

Recipes included and the main ingredients needed

JERRY'S DAD'S BABY PIZZA
English muffins, tomato sauce, pepperoni, green pepper, onions, mushrooms

COLD DORM DRINK
Orange juice, Jello

BAKED-BEAN RAREBIT
Baked beans, American cheese, milk, egg, toast

HAM-AND-APPLE CASSEROLE
Ham, apples, onions, milk

JODI'S BANANA SHAKE
Bananas, milk, honey

JOCKO'S OVEN DELIGHT
Onions, tomatoes, sharp cheese, bread crumbs

DENISE'S TORTILLA CHIP SALAD
Lettuce, ground beef, kidney beans, tomatoes, tortilla chips, cheddar cheese, onion, mayonnaise, chili sauce, pickle relish

WELSH RABBIT
Flour, milk, cheese, toast

WAFFLES
Eggs, flour, sugar, milk

**ERIC'S ALMOST FOOLPROOF
CHOCOLATE SOUFFLE**
Unsweetened chocolate, flour, milk, sugar, eggs,
rum

HOT DORM DRINK
Powdered milk, Nestle's Quick

SMOOTHIES
Bananas, honey, fruit

SUN-BREWED TEA
Tea, water, sun

EGGY HAM TOAST
Ham, cream, egg yolk, toast

From the University of Colorado:

Jerry's Dad's Baby Pizza

Cut English muffins in half. Place in flat pan. Spread
tomato sauce on each half. For each half muffin,
place 3 slices of pepperoni over tomato sauce. Add
slices of green pepper rings, onion rings, sliced
mushrooms. Top with slices of mozzarella cheese.
Bake in 350° F. oven until toasty and melted.

We usually figure 4 halves apiece but we eat large
portions.

From the University of Denver:

Cold Dorm Drink

This is a good drink for dorm residents who have no cooking facilities.

Take an empty jar with a tight-fitting lid. Put in 1 part orange juice, one part powdered Jello (I like raspberry) . . . add cold water from the water fountain. Put on lid and shake it up. Better than a Coke.

From Union College (Schenectady, N.Y.):

Baked - Bean Rarebit

1 cup American cheese, grated
1 cup milk
salt and pepper
¼ teaspoon dry mustard
1 cup baked beans, mashed
1 egg, slightly beaten

Melt butter in pan, stir in cheese, milk, and seasonings gradually until mixture is perfectly smooth. Add beans and egg. Stir and cook till hot (very soon). Serve over toast.

From the University of Texas:

Ham - and - Apple Casserole

Someone makes this in the afternoon so it is all ready to put in the oven an hour before we think we are going to want it.

Equal amount of ham, tart apples, and onions. The ham should be cooked. Slice into buttered casserole in layers, starting with apples. Dot each layer with butter and sprinkle with salt and pepper. Repeat until you have as much as you need to feed whomever will be eating. Pour in milk about ⅔ up the casserole. Top with buttered bread crumbs. An hour before you want to eat, put it in a 400° F. oven and bake covered for 45 minutes, uncovered for 15 minutes.

From Goddard College:

Jodi's Banana Shake

A good pick-up when you need one.

2 cups milk
2 sliced bananas
1 tablespoon honey
dash of cinnamon
almost 1 teaspoon vanilla

Put all ingredients in blender. Then add 1 or 2 ice cubes. Blend until ice is chopped or instead of ice, add two scoops of ice cream . . . chocolate is good.

From Texas Christian University:

Jocko's Oven Delight

This is best made in a round ovenware casserole, 1- or 2-quart size, depending on number of eaters. One quart will serve 3 or 4; 2 quarts (double all quantities) will serve 6 or 8.

To make 1 quart:
3 large onions
4 tomatoes
1 lb. sharp cheese
1 cup buttered bread crumbs

Slice all ingredients thinly. If you don't have a tomato knife, your knife will have to be very sharp to do this successfully. Salt and pepper vegetables.

Layer onions, then cheese, and then tomatoes in casserole until almost full. Bake on middle rack of oven for about 1 hour. Top with bread crumbs and continue baking until crumbs are golden brown.

From the University of Texas:

Denise's Tortilla Chip Salad

1 head lettuce
1 lb. ground beef
¾ teaspoon seasoned salt
½ teaspoon each, onion powder, garlic powder, chili powder
⅛ teaspoon cayenne
4 drops red pepper sauce
⅔ cup water
1 14-oz. can kidney beans, drained
4 tomatoes, cut into eighths
1 6¼-oz. package tortilla chips
1 cup shredded cheddar cheese (about 4 oz.)
1 cup chopped onion
½ cup mayonnaise or salad dressing
¼ cup chili sauce
1 tablespoon pickle relish

Wash lettuce and shred. Chill at least 1 hour.

Brown ground beef in large skillet. Drain. Stir in seasonings, water, and kidney beans. Simmer, uncovered, for 15 minutes, stirring occasionally. Cool 10 minutes.

Combine greens, tomatoes, tortilla chips, and cheese in large salad bowl. Mix together mayonnaise, chili sauce, and pickle relish. Toss gently with salad mixture. Pour warm ground beef mixture over salad. Toss gently. *Serve immediately.*

Serves 8.

From Columbia University:

Welsh Rabbit

Melt 1 tablespoon butter in pan. Add 1 tablespoon flour, mix well. Add ½ cup milk, cook until thick. Add 1 handful of grated cheese . . . cheddar or any leftover cooking cheese you have . . . stir until melted and blended. Add a little dry mustard. Serve over toast. Just enough for 1 person.

From Boston College:

Waffles

When exams start, we make this up in large quantities and refrigerate it; then anyone who gets hungry at odd hours can quickly make waffles. We got a used waffle iron for practically nothing at Goodwill.

Mix:
3 **beaten eggs**
2 **cups flour (best if 1 cup is whole-wheat flour)**
2 **tablespoons baking soda**
1 **tablespoon sugar**
1 **teaspoon vanilla**
4 **tablespoons melted butter**
approximately 1¼ cups milk (add gradually until batter is good consistency for pouring onto waffle iron)

Just before cooking, add 1 cup of mashed bananas or one cup of blueberries.

From the University of Pittsburgh:

Eric's Almost Foolproof Chocolate Soufflé

Eric has a tendency toward the richer things in life. He likes to make chocolate eclairs and this, one of our favorites. It is usually made around 4:00 A.M. of the day I am about to have an exam. Obviously, this takes both of us; me to study until 6:00 A.M., him to cook. It's astonishingly durable. The last one survived a partial cooking, followed by refrigeration for 10 hours before it was finally fully cooked. It was a little heavy on the bottom, but it still had enough energy to soufflé. Eric is just a beginner-cook. He says all he does is follow the recipe, so I suppose others can do it too.

Preheat oven to 350° F.

2 **squares unsweetened chocolate**
3 **tablespoons butter**
2 **tablespoons flour**
¼ **teaspoon salt**
1 **cup milk (can use powdered—
   makes it a little "strong")**
½ **cup sugar**
1 **teaspoon vanilla**
2 **tablespoons rum**
4 **egg yolks**
4 **egg whites, stiffly beaten**

Butter a 2-quart soufflé dish (we use an all-purpose Pyrex casserole). Sprinkle all over with granulated sugar. Melt together chocolate and butter; then blend in flour and salt to make a smooth paste. Add milk, sugar, and vanilla gradually. Cook, stirring constantly, until thick. Cool a little, then add rum, then egg yolks, beating well as you add them. Take off stove. Fold in egg whites (you should be able to turn the bowl of egg whites upside down if they are beaten stiff enough) and pour into baking dish. Set in a pan of hot water and bake for about 45 minutes. Top with whipped cream when you serve it.

Serves 4 for dessert . . . 2 at 4:00 A.M.

From the University of Denver:

Hot Dorm Drink

This is a good drink for dorm residents . . . especially if your water fountain has a heating unit. Great after trucking in the rain from class or when you get chilly studying after midnight.

In a coffee cup, fill ⅓ with powdered milk, add 2 teaspoons Nestle's Quick . . . fill with hot water and stir. To get fancy, add marshmallows (keep these in a jar with a tight lid so they don't get stale . . . get the little ones). It may not sound like much but it's good. Just stir well or the last gulp is too rich.

From William Smith College:

Eggy Ham Toast

2 cups cream
1 egg yolk
1 cup boiled or baked ham, chopped fine
salt and pepper to taste

Scald cream. Beat yolk and add to cream. Stir until mixture thickens. Add chopped ham and cook only until it is hot . . . very soon. Serve on toast.

From the University of Denver:

Smoothies

I got this from some students at the University of California in Santa Barbara. They have a small permanent booth where they sell just this drink . . . usually 10 different kinds on the menu any given day.

bananas
fruit—any kind except dried apples.
    I recommend strawberries.
honey
water

Peel bananas and cut in 3 sections. Freeze it (it won't hurt it and it will keep indefinitely if necessary). Remove from freezer. Put in blender, add fruit, 1 or 2 teaspoons honey, and enough water so blender will operate. Turn on blender. When liquid is smooth, it is ready to drink.

Vary it any way you can think of. Try a little orange juice (it will make it thinner), cinnamon, or nutmeg. If you use fruits that don't have as strong a taste as bananas, you may need to use more of those fruits.

From the University of Denver:

Sun-Brewed Tea

One way to have good tea inexpensively is to let the sun brew it.

Get a gallon jug. Fill with water—spring preferably. Add 3 tablespoons of tea or 3 teabags early in the morning. Put it outside somewhere where it will get the sun all day. It will brew with a unique flavor —the water is kinder because it doesn't bruise the leaves the way boiling water does. Very refreshing.

FOOD FOR FRIENDS
AND OTHER GUESTS

Recipes included and the main ingredients needed

NANCY'S ENCHILADAS
  Tortillas, ground beef, pinto beans, onion, Monterey Jack and cheddar cheeses, enchilada sauce

NANCY'S MEXICAN RICE
  Rice, jalapeño peppers, tomatoes

HOT POTATO SALAD
  Potatoes

HUNGARIAN GOULASH
  Sauerkraut, white wine, stew beef, onions, tomatoes, caraway seeds, sour cream

INDIAN RICE
  Rice, cooked chicken, chicken broth, peanuts, Sultana raisins, curry powder, turmeric, ginger

PAT'S PIZZA
  Yeast, mozzarella cheese, pepperoni or sausage, pizza sauce

SAUTÉED CABBAGE
  Cabbage, cream, caraway seeds

STEVE'S PAELLA
  Chicken, squid, mussels, onions, canned tomatoes, garlic, green peppers, shrimp, sausage, peas, pimientos

BAKED PORK CHOPS WITH HERBS
Pork chops, bread crumbs, thyme, parsley, chives

LULI KEBAB
Ground meat, onions, fresh parsley, lemons, dill

From Middlebury College:

Nancy's Enchiladas

These, plus Mexican Rice (see page 257), will serve 4 to 6 people for less than $2 a person (for 6). If your budget won't stand for that, add more beans in proportion to the meat. The recipe is very forgiving and you can use very little beef and lots more beans, onions, and cheese, if you like. Since the number of people served is limited by the number of tortillas you fill, plan accordingly.

Preheat oven to 350° F.

12　tortillas (frozen are cheapest)
2–3　tablespoons peanut oil
1　lb. ground beef
1　8-oz. can pinto beans
1　medium onion, diced
Monterey Jack and mild cheddar cheese, diced

Sauce:
**1–2　cans hot or mild enchilada sauce *or* 8 oz. chili
　　powder plus 1 small can tomatoes**
2　tablespoons flour
1½　cups water (omit if you use tomatoes)
garlic powder to taste

Brown meat. Drain fat and add beans. Cook until hot.

Heat about ¼″ oil in frying pan and fry each tortilla for a few seconds on each side, but don't allow to get crisp. Place in baking dish, fill with 1–2 spoonfuls bean mixture, some onions, and some cheese, then roll.

Prepare all tortillas the same way. Cover with sauce and sprinkle top with cheese. Bake until cheese melts completely and is bubbly.

Note: To feed more, serve with refried beans as well as Mexican Rice.

From Middlebury College:

Nancy's Mexican Rice

Make rice as usual and mix with 1 can jalepeño peppers and tomatoes. The tomatoes can be fresh and coarsely chopped or canned and well drained. Proportions will vary according to how well seasoned and how moist you want the rice to be.

Serving suggestion: Add a cup of nuts, finely chopped, mix well with the rice, and serve with a tossed salad for an inexpensive supper.

From Johns Hopkins University:

Hot Potato Salad

Quick, good, and filling. Goes with everything from hamburgers to bologna. If you want to make a lot, just double everything.

6 potatoes
¼ cup cider vinegar
3 tablespoons hot water
3 tablespoons sugar
salt and pepper to taste

Boil potatoes in their jackets until easily pierced with a fork. Small potatoes take about 20–25 minutes; larger ones take longer. Don't start poking them too soon or you will break them up.

Drain. Cool until you can handle them. Peel and slice but work quickly so they will stay as warm as possible.

Combine all other ingredients in small saucepan and heat to boiling. Pour over potatoes and toss for a minute over very low heat to get them hot again. Do this very gently or you will have hot diced potatoes.

This is good cold the next day if any is left over.

From Duke University:

Hungarian Goulash

My friends thought I was kidding when I said I was making this—but not after they tasted it.

2 **large cans sauerkraut**
1 **cup white wine**
4 **lbs. stewing beef, cubed**
3 **tablespoons peanut oil**
4 **cups onions, sliced thin**
2 **cups canned tomatoes, chopped**
4 **tablespoons paprika**
1 **tablespoon caraway seeds**
Salt to taste
3 **cups sour cream**

Pour wine over sauerkraut, mix, and put aside.

Heat oil in heavy pot or skillet and brown beef on all sides. Add all other ingredients except sour cream. If too dry, add 1 cup of water. It may be necessary to add more later as it cooks—check every so often to make sure there is enough liquid for cooking and serving.

Simmer, covered, about 1 hour, or until meat is tender. It is better to overcook than to serve tough meat.

Take off the fire and stir in sour cream. Cover and let stand to reheat. (If you put the pot back on the fire and the liquid boils, your sour cream may curdle.) Serves 8–10.

Serving idea: Traditional over egg noodles, but rice works fine if that is handier.

From Northwestern University:

Indian Rice

2 cups rice
3 cups cooked chicken, shredded
5 cups chicken broth
2 cups peanuts, chopped
1½ cups Sultana raisins
1 tablespoon curry powder
2 teaspoons turmeric
1 tablespoon ginger
salt to taste

Combine all ingredients in heavy skillet. Cover and simmer until liquid is absorbed and rice is tender. Takes about ½ hour. Do not lift cover until the half-hour is up, then it's OK to check.

From the University of Connecticut:

Pat's Pizza

Pizzas have become so expensive, we make our own. From start to table this takes approximately 1 hour and 20 minutes—time to wash bowls and listen to some records.

Preheat oven to 400° F.

3 cups flour
1 cup warm water
1 package yeast
1 teaspoon sugar
2 tablespoons oil
8–10 oz. mozzarella cheese
½ lb. ground round or pepperoni or sausage
10 oz. pizza sauce, or make your own

Grease bowl. Mix flour, yeast, and sugar in bowl. Add water, mixing with greased spoon till evenly moist. Add oil gradually. Knead dough on board for 5 minutes. Put back in bowl. Cover and let rise in warm, moist area until double in bulk—takes about 1 hour.

While dough is rising, grate cheese, shred meat if necessary. To make your own pizza sauce, simmer together tomato paste, olive oil, oregano, garlic salt, and salt and pepper.

While dough is rising, all utensils can be cleaned and put away. The baker is left with dough bowl, cheese bowl, and sauce bowl only.

Spread dough evenly and flat on greased jelly roll sheet. Add topping, sauce, and cheese, in that order. Bake on second rack down from the top until cheese browns, about 15–20 minutes.

While pizza is baking, clean other bowls, thereby leaving only jelly roll pan and plates for after-dinner clean-up.

From Syracuse University:

Sautéed Cabbage

Serve this with Sweet-Sour Meatballs (page 112) for a super party. (You'll have to double the meatball recipe.)

1　small head cabbage
2　tablespoons oil
½　cup cream
½　teaspoon dry mustard
3　tablespoons vinegar
¼　cup caraway seeds
salt and pepper to taste

Shred cabbage. Heat oil in large skillet and add cabbage, tossing to coat with oil. Combine vinegar, mustard, caraway seeds, salt and pepper.

Continue tossing cabbage for about 8 minutes, then add vinegar mixture. Toss to blend and heat through. Remove from fire and add cream, tossing to blend. Cover, let stand a few minutes, then serve.

Serves 8–10.

From Cornell University:

Steve's Paella

The main ingredients can be changed according to what is cheapest at the time. Pork can substitute for chicken, clams for mussels, some white fish for shrimp. You can use all meat or all fish, and so forth. The seasoning and rice should stay the same.

1 frying chicken, cut up
3 lbs. squid, cleaned and sliced into rings
4–5 dozen mussels, scrubbed and de-bearded
2 onions, minced
1 large can tomatoes
3 garlic cloves, minced
2 green peppers, cut in strips
1 lb. shrimp
¾ cup olive oil
3 lbs. mild sausage
2 cups peas
a pinch of saffron or enough turmeric to color rice
5 cups rice
5 pimientos, sliced in strips
salt to taste

In really large skillet (or paella pan if you have one) fry chicken and sausages until brown. Add tomatoes, garlic, and green pepper and simmer 10 minutes. Add all other ingredients, except fish and shellfish, and 10 cups of hot water. Stir to mix thoroughly. Cook, covered, until rice is almost done, about 20 minutes. Add fish and shellfish, laying them on top of mixture. Cook until shrimp turn pink and mussels open, about 10 minutes. (Be sure to discard any mussels that don't open.)

From the University of Virginia:

Baked Pork Chops with Herbs

Serve this recipe with baked sweet potatoes and vegetables topped with a pat of butter and sealed in foil and you have a delicious meal—all made at the same time and no work.

Preheat oven to 400° F.

8 pork chops, not too thick
4 cups bread crumbs, freshly made
½ cup peanut or safflower oil
3 tablespoons thyme
1 cup parsley, minced
4 tablespoons garlic salt
1½ cups chives, chopped
salt and pepper to taste

Trim excess fat from chops.

Combine all other ingredients and mix thoroughly. One by one, press pork chops down on bread-crumb mix, coating both sides of chop.

Lay chops in a single layer on foil-covered pan. If any bread crumbs are left when you finish, add them to the top of the pork chops, pressing the mixture down onto the top of the chops.

Bake for 1 hour.

From the University of Michigan:

Luli Kebab

Skewered hamburger is different—and makes a great party with salad and French bread.

3 lbs. ground meat (lamb is better but beef is OK)
3 onions, minced
1 cup fresh parsley, minced
2 tablespoons lemon rind, grated
1 tablespoon paprika
1 tablespoon garlic salt
2 tablespoons dill, minced (optional)
½ cup lemon juice

Combine all ingredients, except lemon juice, in a bowl. Mix thoroughly with your hands. Roll into small balls and thread on bamboo skewers. (You can buy them cheaply in bundles of 100.)

Shape each ball around the skewer so it looks more like a hot dog than a ball. Put on as many as the skewer will hold, but keep them all the same thickness so they will cook evenly.

Pour lemon juice over the skewered meat. Arrange on a rack in a broiler pan and broil. When serving, pour the pan juices over the meat, unless the hamburger is too fat. In that case, serve without gravy but with a bowl of plain yogurt.

INDEX

Apple and Ham Casserole, 246
Apple Crisp, 240
Apple Custard, Colonial, 233
Applesauce, 237

Baked-Bean Rarebit, 245
Banana Bread, Yoga, 67
Banana Shake, Jodi's, 246
Beans, Green, in Tomato Sauce, 181
Beans, Green, Sautéed, 183
Beans, Green, Tangy, 182
Beans, Green, Therese's Sister's Gourmet, 182
Beans, Green, with Sour Cream, 184
Beans, Kidney, Mike's Chili, 109
Beans, Pinto, and Beef, 114
Beans, Red, Rice and Beef, 118
Bean Salad, 216
Beef, Ground, and Pinto Beans, 114
Beef, Red Beans and Rice, 118
Beef Casserole, Brazilian, 126
Beef Liver, Scandinavian, 125
Beef Soup, Lynn's Vegetable, 82
Beef Stew, Susannah's, 127

Beef Stroganoff, 116
Bread, 64
Bread, Brown, 73
Bread, Cuban Water Variation, 66
Bread, Molly Hall's, 70
Bread, My, 68
Bread, Yoga Banana, 67
Bread-and-Cheese Casserole, Patty's, 95
Brownies, Butterscotch, 237
Burgers, Tasty, 114
Butter Dips, 71
Butter Sauces, 225
Butterscotch Brownies, 237

Cabbage, Fried Chinese, 186
Cabbage, Sautéed, 262
Cabbage, Sweet-and-Sour Stuffed, 150
Cabbage Casserole, Viennese, 186
Cabbage Soup, Peter's, 77
Cake, Fruit Cocktail, 236
Cake, New England Cheese, 234
Cake, Yum Yum, 242
Carrot Pudding, 97

Carrots, Zingy, 200
Carrots and Yams, Baked, 194
Casserole, Apple and Ham, 246
Casserole, Brazilian Beef, 126
Casserole, Bread-and-Cheese, 95
Casserole, Cheeseburger, 116
Casserole, Enchilada, 113
Casserole, Hamburger Noodle, 120
Casserole, Orange-Yam, 198
Casserole, Potato and Egg, 98
Casserole, Quick-and-Easy, 196
Casserole, Salmon and Mushroom, 177
Casserole, Spinach and Mushroom, 192
Casserole, Swedish, 123
Casserole, Tunafish, 176
Casserole, Viennese Cabbage, 186
Cheese-and-Bread Casserole, 95
Cheeseburger Casserole, 116
Cheese Cake, New England, 234
Cheese Soufflé, Lesley's, 99
Chef's Salad, 219
Chicken, Carol's Barbecued, 161
Chicken, Ellen's Sesame, 162
Chicken, Garlic, 167
Chicken, Mable Desmond's, 163
Chicken, Marinated, 161
Chicken, New Orleans, 164
Chicken, Noralyn's, 162
Chicken, Pineapple, 165
Chicken and Mushrooms, Pam's, 158

Chicken and Olives, 158
Chicken and Tomatoes, Eric's, 168
Chicken Cacciatore, Elaine's, 157
Chicken Cordon Bleu, Charlie's, 159
Chicken Curry, Easy, 155
Chicken Livers and Tomatoes, 160
Chicken Soup, Nanny's, 81
Chicken Veronique, Charles's, 156
Chili, Fairly Cheap, 106
Chili, Mike's, 109
Chocolate-Chip Toast, 242
Chocolate Soufflé, Eric's Almost Foolproof, 250
Chowder, New England Cod, 78
Cinnamon Puffs, Hot, 72
Clam Sauce, 225
Clam Spaghetti, 207
Cocido, 104
Cod Chowder, New England, 78
Coleslaw, 218
Coleslaw, Lynn's, 218
Cookies, Granola, 238
Couscous, Libyan, 146
Cucumbers, Fried, 188
Curry Sauce, 226
Custard, Colonial Apple, 233

Danish Barbecue Hamburgers, 119
Date Candy Fudge, 238
Dorm Drink, Cold, 245
Dorm Drink, Hot, 251
Dressing, Salad, Finest, 228
Dressing, Salad, German, 229

Dressing, Salad, Sour-Cream, 227
Dressing, Salad, II, 228

Egg and Potato Casserole, 98
Egg Foo Yong, 92
Eggplant, Broiled, 188
Eggplant Eggs, 96
Eggplant Parmigiana, 187
Eggs, Chinese, 101
Eggs, Eggplant, 96
Eggs, Fried, 88
Eggs, Hard-Cooked, 87
Eggs, Herbed Scrambled, 90
Eggs, Poached, 89
Eggs, Soft-Cooked, 87
Egg Salad, 93
Eggs Richard, 100
Eggy Ham Toast, 252
Enchilada Casserole, 113
Enchiladas, Nancy's, 256

Fish, Baked Herbed, 176
Fish Fillets in White Wine, 170
Fish Scallop, 171
Flounder in Sour Cream, Baked, 174
Fruit Cocktail Cake, 236
Fruit Soup, Hot, 83
Fruit Yogurt, 233
Fudge, Date Candy, 238

Gazpacho, 80
Goulash, Hungarian, 259
Granola, Danny's, 61
Granola, Jodi's, 60
Granola, Mike's, 57
Granola, Minnesota Multi, 58
Granola, Sue's, 59

Granola Cookies, 238
Gravy or Brown Sauce, 226
Grinders, Shari's, 111
Guacamole, 219

Haddock, Baked Stuffed, 173
Ham-and-Apple Casserole, 246
Hamburger Noodle Casserole, 120
Hamburgers, Danish Barbecue, 119
Hamburgers Hawaiian, 106
Ham Toast, Eggy, 252
Hot Pot, English, 144

Jambalaya, Patty's, 175
Jocko's Oven Delight, 247

Lamb, Breast of, Barbecued, 145
Lamb Curry with Yogurt, 141
Lamb Stew, Easy, 140
Lamb Stew, English, 143
Lamb Stew, Irish, 142
Lasagna, Jodi's, 212
Lasagna, Kim's, 210
Lemon Butter Sauce, 225
Lemon Cheese Pie, 240
Liver, Scandinavian Beef, 125
Lubi and Rice, 149
Luli Kebab, 265

Macaroni and Cheese, Super-Quick, 213
Marinade, Wine, 228
Meatballs, Sweet-Sour, 112
Meat Loaf, 107
Moussaka, 148

Mushroom and Salmon Casserole, 177
Mushroom and Spinach Casserole, 192
Mushrooms, Sue's Stuffed, 190
Mushrooms and Veal, 134
Mushroom Sauce, 226

Omelet, Onion, 91
Omelette, James's, 90
Onion Sauce, 225, 227
Onion Soup, Cream of, 79
Orange-Onion Salad, 220
Orange-Yam Casserole, 198
Osso Buco, 132

Paella, Steve's, 262
Palacsinta, Hungarian, 94
Pancake, Potato, 192
Peanut Butter, Carob Goo Candy, 241
Pea Soup, Split, 84
Pepper Ballies, 108
Peppers, Stuffed, 108
Pie, Lemon Cheese, 240
Pie Filling, Yogurt, 235
Pineapple Chicken, 165
Pizza, Jerry's Dad's Baby, 244
Pizza, Pat's, 260
Popovers, 69
Pork Chops, Baked, with Herbs, 264
Potato and Egg Casserole, 98
Potato Pancake, 192
Potato Salad, Chilled, 217
Potato Salad, Hot, 216, 258
Potato Salad with Yogurt, 221
Pudding, Carrot, 97
Pudding, Rice, 239

Pudding, Spinach, 191
Puffs, Hot Cinnamon, 72

Quick-and-Easy Casserole, 196
Quick-Fry Vegetables, 195

Rarebit, Baked-Bean, 245
Ratatouille, 189
Relish, Turkish Eggplant, 188
Rice, Basic Brown, and Vegetables, 203
Rice, Fried, 205
Rice, Indian, 260
Rice, Nancy's Mexican, 257
Rice, Red Beans and Beef, 118
Rice, Savory, 211
Rice, Yellow, 204
Rice Patties, Brown, 206
Rice Pudding, 239

Salmon and Mushroom Casserole, 177
Sauce, Cheese, 227
Sauce, Clam, 225
Sauce, Curry, 225, 226
Sauce, Gravy or Brown, 226
Sauce, Lemon Butter, 225
Sauce, Mushroom, 226
Sauce, Onion, 225, 227
Sauce, White, 226
Sauces, Butter, 225
Shish Kabob Without the Kabob, 124
Shrimp 'n' Rice, 172
Smoothies, 252
Snickers, 232
Soufflé, Eric's Almost Foolproof Chocolate, 250
Soufflé, Lesley's Cheese, 99

Sour Cream Salad Dressing, 227
Spaghetti, Clam, 207
Spaghetti with Homemade Meat Sauce, 209
Spinach and Mushroom Casserole, 192
Spinach Pudding, 191
Spinach with Sour Cream, 193
Spoonburgers, 115
Steak, Ground, Chinese Pepper, 110
Stew, Easy Lamb, 140
Stew, English Lamb, 143
Stew, Irish Lamb, 142
Stew, Susannah's Beef, 122
Stockpot, Alice's, 76
Swedish Casserole, 123

Tacos, 121
Tea, Sun-Brewed, 253
Toast, Chocolate-Chip, 242
Tobouli, 220
Tomatoes and Chicken Livers, 160
Tomato-Zucchini Quickie, 196
Tortilla Chip Salad, Denise's, 248
Tunafish Casserole, 176
Tuna-Vegetable Mix, 174
Turkey, Roast, 166

Veal, Breast of, and Mushrooms, 134
Veal, Breast of, Stuffed, 133
Veal, Breast of, Sunday-Best, 130
Veal and Mushrooms, 134
Veal and Tomatoes, Sautéed, 137

Veal Parmesan, 135
Veal Patties, Breaded, 129
Veal Patties in Sour Cream, 131
Veal Teriyaki, 136
Vegetarian Dishes, see page 178.

Waffles, 249
Welsh Rabbit, 249
Wine Marinade, 228

Yam-Orange Casserole, 198
Yams, Baked Carrots and, 194
Yams, Left-Over (or Not) Baked, 199
Yams, Velvet, 199
Yogurt Fruit, 233
Yogurt Pie Filling, 235
Yum Yum Cake, 242

Zucchini, Shredded, 197
Zucchini Bread, Tillie Taylor's, 65
Zucchini Dinner in a Dish, 117
Zucchini-Tomato Quickie, 196

**The following dishes are
all vegetarian:**

Baked-Bean Rarebit, 245
Bean Salad, 216
Beans, Green, in Tomato Sauce, 181
Beans, Green, Sautéed, 183
Beans, Green, Therese's Sister's Gourmet, 182
Beans, Green, with Sour Cream, 184
Bread-and-Cheese Casserole, 95

Cabbage, Fried Chinese, 186
Cabbage, Sautéed, 262
Cabbage Casserole, Viennese, 186
Cabbage Soup, Peter's, 77
Carrot Pudding, 97
Carrots, Zingy, 200
Carrots and Yams, Baked, 194
Cheese Soufflé, Lesley's, 99
Coleslaw, 218
Coleslaw, Lynn's, 218
Cucumbers, Fried, 188

Egg and Potato Casserole, 98
Egg Foo Yong, 92
Eggplant, Broiled, 188
Eggplant Eggs, 96
Eggplant Parmigiana, 187
Eggplant Relish, Turkish, 188
Eggs, Fried, 88
Eggs, Hard-Cooked, 87
Eggs, Herbed Scrambled, 90
Eggs, Poached, 89
Eggs, Soft-Cooked, 87
Egg Salad, 93
Eggs Richard, 100

Fruit Soup, Hot, 83

Gazpacho, 80
Guacamole, 219

Inspiration Salad, 222

Jocko's Oven Delight, 247

Macaroni and Cheese, Super-Quick, 213
Mushrooms, Sue's Stuffed, 190

Omelet, Onion, 91
Omelette, James's, 90

Onion Soup, Cream of, 79
Orange-Onion Salad, 220
Orange-Yam Casserole, 198

Palacsinta, Hungarian, 94
Pizza, Jerry's Dad's Baby, 244
Potato Pancake, 192
Potato Salad, Chilled, 217
Potato Salad, Hot, 258
Potato Salad with Yogurt, 221

Quick-and-Easy Casserole, 196

Ratatouille, 189
Rice, Fried, 205
Rice, Nancy's Mexican, 257
Rice and Vegetables, Basic Brown, 203
Rice Patties, Brown, 206

Spaghetti Alla Carbonara, 208
Spinach-and-Mushroom Casserole, 192
Spinach Pudding, 191
Spinach with Sour Cream, 193
Stockpot, Alice's, 76

Tobouli, 220

Vegetables, Quick-Fry, 195
Vegetables, Scalloped, 185
Vegetable Soup, Simple, 76

Waffles, 249
Welsh Rabbit, 249

Yams, Left-Over (or Not), 199
Yams, Velvet, 199

Zucchini, Shredded, 197
Zucchini-Tomato Quickie, 196